SERGEI
RACHMANINOV

CLASSIC *f*M
LIFELINES

SERGEI
RACHMANINOV

AN ESSENTIAL GUIDE
TO HIS LIFE AND WORKS

JULIAN HAYLOCK

PAVILION

First published in Great Britain in 1996 by
PAVILION BOOKS LIMITED
26 Upper Ground, London SE1 9PD

Edited and designed by Castle House Press, Llantrisant, South Wales
Cover designed by Bet Ayer

A CIP catalogue record for this book is available
from the British Library

ISBN 1 85793 944 1

Set in Lydian and Caslon
Printed and bound in Great Britain by Mackays of Chatham

2 4 6 8 10 9 7 5 3 1

This book can be ordered direct from the publisher.
Please contact the Marketing Department.
But try your bookshop first.

Contents

ACKNOWLEDGMENTS

To my wife, Barbara, and daughter, Stephanie,
for 'keeping the coffee on the boil' and
for making every day so special

In Memory of Sophia Satin
for all her help and kindness
in the preparation of this book

With grateful thanks to Eileen Townsend Jones of Castle House Press, whose boundless expertise and enthusiasm were a constant source of inspiration throughout the writing of this book.

To find out more about Rachmaninov, contact:
The Rachmaninoff Society (President: Vladimir Ashkenazy),
4 Springfield Cottages, New Road, Rotherfield, East Sussex TN6 3JR

A NOTE FROM THE EDITORS

A biography of this type inevitably contains numerous references to pieces of music. The paragraphs are also peppered with 'quotation marks', since much of the tale is told through reported speech.

Because of this, and to make things more accessible for the reader as well as easier on the eye, we decided to simplify the method of typesetting the names of musical works. Conventionally this is determined by the nature of the individual work, following a set of rules whereby some pieces appear in italics, some in italics and quotation marks, others in plain roman type and others still in roman and quotation marks.

In this book, the names of all musical works are simply set in italics. Songs and arias appear in italics and quotation marks.

CHAPTER I
FROM ST PETERSBURG TO MOSCOW
(1873–88)

- ◆ *Early childhood*
- ◆ *Move to St Petersburg*
- ◆ *Moscow Conservatory*
- ◆ *Enter Zverev*
- ◆ *First compositions*

S ergei Vasilyevich Rachmaninov (1873–1943) was the last in the line of great Romantic pianist-composers that had begun so spectacularly with Franz Liszt and Fryderyk Chopin. Throughout a career lasting half a century, he seldom wavered from his richly melodious composing style, despite being scoffingly dismissed as a musical dinosaur by many of his contemporaries. An outwardly austere and reserved figure – 'a six-and-a-half-foot scowl', Stravinsky called him – he scarcely ever allowed the mask to drop in public.

Composing, on the other hand, was a burning imperative, a psychological safety valve. Rarely given to explanation or self-justification, in later life Rachmaninov nailed his colours firmly to the mast:

> *A composer's music should express the country of his birth, his love affairs, his religion, the books that have influenced him, the pictures he loves. It should be the sum total of a composer's experience.*

It is easy to imagine the howls of derisive laughter with which such open sincerity would have been met in some quarters. Yet it is Rachmaninov's concertos and symphonies that continue to play to full houses, while some of the most innovative music of his time is still struggling to find a general audience.

Musicianship in Rachmaninov's family already went back at least three generations on his father's side. His officer grandfather, Arkady, could even boast of having once had piano lessons with the Irish émigré virtuoso and composer John Field. However, given the family's strong military traditions, Arkady was delighted when his sixteen-year-old son Vasily (Sergei's father) announced his intention to join the Imperial Army.

Vasily, a strictly amateur pianist, revelled in the riotous social life of the armed forces. He enjoyed his liquor and women, gambled heavily, and following his decommission lost no time in marrying Lyubov Boutakova, a wealthy general's daughter. She brought with her a hefty five estates as a wedding dowry, amounting to many hundreds of acres of breathtaking, undulating scenery. The couple settled at Oneg, a gloriously spacious holding about an hour's journey from Novgorod, and had three children in fairly quick succession – two daughters, Yelena and Sofiya, and a son, Vladimir.

Outwardly the marriage appeared secure enough, but trouble was brewing. Vasily had lost a small fortune on a series of hairbrained financial ventures, and by the early 1870s he had already been forced to sell off three of the family's precious estates.

It was against this rapidly downward-spiralling financial position that on 20 March 1873, Lyubov gave birth to their second son, Sergei Vasilyevich. Shortly afterwards, yet another estate was sold, forcing Vasily temporarily to curb his spending excesses. Lyubov had two more children – Vavara, who died in infancy, and a son, Arkady.

The family unit muddled along, although Lyubov constantly struggled to cope, both with the children's growing demands and with Vasily's charming indifference to the situation. Nevertheless, she was quick to recognize and encourage Rachmaninov's obvious musical ability. In later life, he remembered being occasionally made to sit under the piano stool as a 'punishment'. Yet, by the age of six, he was already revelling in his first formal piano lessons with the gifted and highly personable Anna Ornatskaya, a distinguished graduate of the St Petersburg Conservatory.

Rachmaninov was by all accounts a contented child, prone to a certain mischievousness – an attractive and beguiling characteristic that endured into maturity. The wide expanses of the country estate were a constant source of pleasure, and the tolling of bells held a powerful fascination for him from an early age. Bells were a part of everyday life in rural Russia, not only marking the passing of time, but also as calls to worship. Their various intonations became intimately associated in Rachmaninov's mind with a whole range of childhood experiences, some pleasant, others rather more distressing. According to Oskar von Riesemann's volume of *Recollections*, one particularly grand funeral in Novgorod Cemetery, accompanied by the relentless tolling of huge iron bells, stamped itself eternally on his memory.

Family life suited Rachmaninov, yet although he was utterly devoted to his brothers and sisters, his attitude towards his father was decidedly ambivalent. Even as a young child he was distantly aware of Vasily's roguish indifference, although the latter was always truly affectionate towards the children. Lyubov bore the brunt of the responsibility for their upkeep, but despite her caring attempts to shield them from any marital tension, she was less forthcoming on the emotional front.

In 1881, Rachmaninov's near-idyllic childhood came to an abrupt halt. Vasily's continuing financial recklessness had inevitably resulted in the sale of the Oneg estate, and with it their home. The family was forced to move out and away from the countryside, settling in a small flat in an unpleasant suburb of St Petersburg. Rachmaninov's older brother, Vladimir, gained immediate entry to a military school, while ten-year-old Sergei won a music scholarship to study at the junior department of the St Petersburg Conservatory in 1883.

The celebrations were comparatively short-lived, for, together with Vladimir and Sofiya, he succumbed to the diphtheria epidemic that was then raging throughout the great city. The boys eventually pulled through, but Sofiya never regained consciousness. Rachmaninov, already distressed by the move and colossal change in circumstances, was deeply traumatized by this loss. His inconsolable fear of death was later to become a polarizing force in his music, encapsulated by frequent references to the haunting *Dies Irae* (Day of Wrath) chant.

Sofiya's death was the final straw for Lyubov, who considered it the direct outcome of Vasily's lack of financial discipline and the family's enforced move to St Petersburg. For his part, Vasily was filled with remorse for his actions, although a split eventually became inevitable. The couple decided merely to separate, as divorce was a complex procedure and generally frowned upon by Russian orthodoxy – they never saw each other again.

Outwardly, Rachmaninov appeared largely unaffected by what was going on, typically choosing to suffer in silence; this rare ability would hold him in great stead throughout his life.

Lyubov was now left without a regular source of income, and had sole responsibility for four children. In desperation, she contacted her mother, Madame Sofiya Boutakova, who promptly made the arduous sixty-mile journey northwards from Novgorod to see what she could do to help out. Showing every conceivable kindness, and positively doting on Rachmaninov's extraordinary musical gifts, she even went as far as to purchase a farm for the family, at Borisovo, just outside Novgorod.

Rachmaninov became particularly attached to his grandmother, who provided a release for his pent-up feelings, and before long came to represent the mother figure that he had never really enjoyed until then. They attended countless church services together – the sound of bells and *a capella* (unaccompanied) singing in the churches and monasteries of the Novgorod region were a continual source of inspiration for Rachmaninov. Following such encounters, he would set about playing on the piano the chants he had heard, invariably receiving a small coin as a reward. It is hardly a coincidence that his finest melodies have a tendency towards long-winding, stepwise motion, an essential characteristic of ancient Russian chant.

The overwhelming wave of emotional fulfilment and self-confidence that resulted from all this devoted attention soon began to play havoc with Rachmaninov's young emotions. He began skipping lessons at the Conservatory, and, astonishingly, managed to keep up the deception for several terms simply by doctoring his increasingly negative end-of-term reports.

The situation finally came to a head at the end of the 1885 spring term. He had failed in all his general subjects, and Lyubov was formally asked to withdraw him from the Conservatory. At her wits' end to know what to do with the boy, she got in touch with her twenty-one-year-old nephew, Alexander Siloti.

Siloti, one of Liszt's star piano pupils, was well aware of Rachmaninov's exceptional musical ability, and suggested he be moved instead to the Moscow Conservatory. Furthermore, he promised to ensure that Rachmaninov would receive the kind of disciplined regime that until that time had clearly been lacking both at home and in his education. Siloti knew just the right man for the job: his own former professor at the Conservatory, the formidable Nikolai Zverev.

In the autumn of 1885, it was a forlorn and desolate twelve-year-old who left for Moscow to take up his lodgings at Zverev's home. Earlier in the day, Rachmaninov had made one last visit to a convent service with his grandmother, who had then seen him safely onto the train, having stitched one hundred roubles into the lining of his coat.

Rachmaninov was greeted at Moscow's vast central station by his aunt Julia (Siloti's mother), with whom he spent the first couple of days being shown all the sights and sounds of the great city. After this brief chance to acclimatize himself to his new surroundings, he was introduced to his mentor-to-be. From now on he would share Zverev's apartment with two other gifted pupils, Matvey Pressman and Leonid Maximov.

Immediately Rachmaninov felt the change in intellectual climate. Gone forever were the halcyon days of fun and games while playing truant from the St Petersburg Conservatory – he now received a rigorous, all-embracing training as a potential concert pianist. The three boys were expected to practise for a minimum of three hours a day, taking it in turns for the early-morning shift under the watchful eye of Zverev's spinster sister, Anna. In addition, there were the usual formal lessons at the Conservatory, personally monitored by Zverev.

Life with the fifty-three-year-old Zverev was highly demanding and strictly regimented, yet everything had its purpose and he was no mere disciplinarian. Indeed, for those who could stand the pace, he offered a remarkable form of musical education. Despite the intensely claustrophobic environment, any potential discomfort appears to have been more than compensated for by the comprehensiveness and sheer variety of Zverev's regime. This included regular trips to the theatre, ballet and opera, as well as dining out at some of the city's most exclusive restaurants. Zverev was also particularly keen on gypsy music, and this had an unmistakable impact on the highly impressionable Rachmaninov's earliest pieces.

Distinguished musicians, including Siloti and the composer, Pyotr Tchaikovsky, would often call in at Zverev's flat. They would play a little, stay to dinner, and then settle down to an impromptu soirée given by the three gifted pupils, or 'cubs' as Zverev affectionately called them. Rachmaninov later recollected:

> *I can barely describe how inspiring it was to perform in front of the finest musicians in Moscow, and to receive such distinguished encouragement.*

It was during the summer of 1886 that Rachmaninov appears to have made his first tentative attempt at serious composition – a piano piece unfortunately now lost. Rachmaninov's fellow 'cub', Matvey Pressman, later recalled the event, no doubt with a fair degree of poetic license:

> *When he was sure there was no one else about, he [Rachmaninov] called me over to the piano and started playing. 'Do you know what this is?' he asked. 'No,' I replied, 'I don't recognize it at all.' 'And what do you think of this pedal point in the bass held against this chromatic progression?' I nodded my approval. 'I composed it myself,' he announced proudly, 'and I dedicate it to you.'*

Another missing manuscript dating from the same period is a piano-duet transcription of Tchaikovsky's '*Manfred*' Symphony, a considerable undertaking that Rachmaninov and Pressman later played to the great man himself. Tchaikovsky was by now something of a musical hero for the young composer, and this early encounter was clearly inspirational:

> *To him I owe the first and possibly the deciding success in my life. Tchaikovsky, at that time, was already world famous, and honoured by everybody, but he remained unspoilt. He was one of the most charming artists and men I ever met. . . . He was modest, as all truly great people are, and simple, as very few are.*

The piano dominated Rachmaninov's creative thinking from the start. Even his early piano pieces of 1887 reveal the extraordinary sense of kinship he felt with the instrument. His first surviving piece, the *Song without Words in D minor*, already evokes the same kind of wistful nostalgia that was to recur with greater intensity in his mature work. The three *Nocturnes* also point the way forward, their gentle borrowings from Tchaikovsky, Schumann and Chopin occasionally erupting in an almost Lisztian frenzy.

Encouraged by the success of the *Nocturnes* in particular, Rachmaninov immediately set to work on an orchestral *Scherzo*, ambitiously headed 'third movement'. For once, it is not Tchaikovsky who first comes to mind as one listens to this promising student work, but the equivalent movement of Mendelssohn's incidental music to *A Midsummer Night's Dream*.

Rachmaninov, meanwhile, had begun the autumn term of 1888 with a new piano teacher: his devoted cousin, Alexander Siloti. Such was his astonishing rate of progress that following his end-of-year examination, Rachmaninov was entered in the Conservatory register as having achieved a '5+', the highest possible mark. Tchaikovsky, as external assessor, had excitedly added three further '+' signs above, below and beside the official figure – a moving tribute from Russia's greatest living composer to the man destined to carry his mantle into the next century.

Rachmaninov was now on something of a personal 'high'. However, his mounting urge to specialize in composition rather than the piano was already causing problems with the notoriously inflexible Zverev. The decision had to be taken either to continue under the old man's strict guidance, or to take charge of his own destiny.

CHAPTER 2
EARLY SUCCESS AND A CATASTROPHIC PREMIERE
(1889–97)

- ♦ *Break with Zverev*
- ♦ *Ivanovka*
- ♦ *Awarded Great Gold Medal*
- ♦ *First published works*
- ♦ *C sharp minor Prelude*
- ♦ *Failure of First Symphony*

Rachmaninov's enthusiasm for composing and his desire for creative freedom were now on a collision course with Zverev's strict routine and discipline. The final eruption came in the autumn of 1889, when a heated exchange took place during which Zverev raised a fist at his disciple. This impetuous gesture resulted in a total breakdown of relations. Rachmaninov tried to make amends by waiting outside the Conservatory on several occasions, but, deeply distressed by the whole affair, Zverev ignored him.

Zverev had opened up a whole new world of professional music-making to the budding young composer. He had also made a tremendous personal impact: Rachmaninov's somewhat reserved manner had been consciously derived from the Zverev role-model. Yet the old man's stubbornness made any further discussion impossible, despite further attempts to patch things up. Rachmaninov reluctantly moved out of Zverev's lodgings, finally settling in with his aunt Vavara Satina and her two young daughters.

The summer was spent with the Satins on their estate at Ivanovka, about 100 kilometres from Tambov, south-east of Moscow. This later became Rachmaninov's own home, and the place where many of his greatest works would be conceived. Here, he also met his cousins, Natalia, Ludmilla and Vera Skalon, for the first time. The sisters found his natural shyness and intensity a little hard going at first, but were entirely won over by his music.

Rachmaninov quickly became an enthusiastic convert to the wide open expanses of Ivanovka, having at first missed the undulating landscapes around Novgorod that he had so enjoyed as a child. He later reflected in his memoirs: 'This estate resembled a boundless ocean, where the waves are endless fields of wheat, rye and oats, stretching as far as the eye can see.'

Inspired by his new surroundings and such appealing and appreciative company, Rachmaninov gave vent to his emotions by composing the first movement of what was his most important and largest work to date: the *First Piano Concerto*, Op.1 (completed in 1892). In addition, he wrote the deeply expressive *Romance in F minor* for cello and piano, dedicating it to Vera Skalon, who at fifteen was the youngest of the sisters and the one to whom Rachmaninov had taken a particular shine.

Indeed, so obvious was the strength of his feelings that Aunt Vavara felt compelled to put a stop to things, and forbade him to write to Vera after his return to Moscow. However, Rachmaninov managed to get round the problem by sustaining some degree of correspondence at one step removed through Natalia Skalon. It would seem that she also felt a strong attraction to the charismatic teenage composer, but, as with the majority of Rachmaninov's relationships with women, just how aware he was of her feelings for him, and whether they were reciprocated, is swathed in obscurity. Perhaps the strongest indication is her severing of relations with Rachmaninov following his marriage to Natalia Satina in 1902.

Two contemporary reminiscences by fellow Conservatory students create a strong impression of the budding young composer on the crest of this initial wave of creative success, the first from Nikolai Avierino:

> *I believe I am not wrong in suggesting that at the age of seventeen or eighteen, Rachmaninov had a fully developed personality. He was self-assured but not arrogant, he held himself with dignity, and was always perfectly happy to join in, although he didn't appear to fraternize with anyone in particular.*

Mikhail Bukinik's observations form part of a general reflection on life at the Moscow Conservatory, which emphasize Rachmaninov's rather reserved nature and the awe in which he was held by many of his comrades:

> *And in this gathering, there is Sergei Rachmaninov. Tall and gaunt, his broad shoulders give him a rectangular appearance. His long face is highly expressive.... His hair is unruly (not yet closely clipped).... He smokes incessantly, speaks with a deep voice, and although he is our exact contemporary, seems somehow a great deal older. Everyone knows about the brilliant new pieces he composes for Professor Arensky, his profound structural instincts, extraordinary sight-reading ability, perfect pitch, and infectious enthusiasm for Tchaikovsky's music.... But his piano playing is perhaps not quite in the same league.*

Rachmaninov began the new year (1891) in full flow, with his exhilarating *Russian Rhapsody* for two pianos – composed in the form of a theme and eight variations, and completed in just three days. The theme itself has an untypically 'folkish' feel to it, and the self-conscious brilliance of the succeeding variations suggests that this was a piece written primarily to display his own virtuosity. It was around this time that Rachmaninov first emerged with a daring new cropped hairstyle, which so delighted his friends and family that he kept it to the end of his days.

A feud between Rachmaninov's piano teacher, Alexander Siloti, and the recently appointed Conservatory Director, Vasily Safanov, had meanwhile come to a head. Siloti could no longer tolerate Safanov's dictatorial methods and resigned immediately. This left Rachmaninov with the difficult choice of either accepting a change of piano teacher for his graduation year, or taking his piano finals a year early. Safanov agreed to the latter, and Rachmaninov furiously set to work, preparing the regulation Chopin *B minor Sonata* first movement, and Beethoven's '*Appassionata*' *Sonata*, in an unbelievable three weeks, just in time for the examination. On 24 May, he graduated with honours.

Alexander Goldenweiser, a fellow pupil, later recalled Rachmaninov's prodigious pianistic talent:

> *Rachmaninov's talent ... surpassed any other in my experience –*

almost unbelievable, like the young Mozart. He memorized new
pieces at an almost unprecedented rate. I recall how Siloti,
our piano teacher, asked Rachmaninov to study Brahms's fa-
mous Variations and Fugue on a Theme of Handel. *This*
was on a Wednesday, and only three days later Rachmaninov
was already playing them from memory like a master. . . .

Rachmaninov spent a quiet summer at Ivanovka with Siloti, where he composed and scored the remainder of his *First Piano Concerto* in a remarkable two-and-a-half days. Although today's audiences are mostly familiar with the wholesale revision he made in 1917, this feat is a demonstration of the young composer's extraordinary flair and lyrical instincts. Listening to this impassioned, brilliant music, articulated by countless individual turns of phrase, it is difficult to credit it as being the work of a mere nineteen-year-old, especially as Rachmaninov had so far given little indication that he could have handled such an ambitious project so successfully. Most significantly, we now see that he showed a remarkable instinct for communicating a heightened sense of rapture with a potency matched by few other composers.

Firing on all creative cylinders, Rachmaninov set to work on the first movement of an intended *Symphony in D minor*. However, a quick dip in the freezing river Matir caused a severe chill, which brought the project to an abrupt halt. When at one point he briefly relapsed into a coma, relatives and friends feared the worst. Meanwhile, during short periods of consciousness, Rachmaninov finished the movement – and, despite the extraordinary circumstance of its completion, it shows a major advance in style over the *Scherzo* of 1888. The orchestral forces are handled with increased confidence and security, yet there is no mistaking the profound influence of Tchaikovsky, and in particular the latter's *Fourth Symphony*.

Fully recovered, Rachmaninov rounded off the year in style with his first orchestral symphonic poem, *Prince Rostislav*, composed in just over a week. Based on the ballad by Alexei Tolstoy, it tells of a soldier who having been killed in battle, cries out to his family from beyond the grave. His calls go unheard and he resigns himself to lie forgotten at the bottom of the river Dnieper. This unfairly neglected piece is more individual in expression than the recent symphonic movement. Rachmaninov's ability to translate pictorial images into musical sound is well illustrated here by some highly effective string writing that uncannily suggests the river's ebb and flow. After a final, maniacal climax, the music subsides, exhausted. This memorable ending anticipates a similar passage in the *Isle of the Dead*, written 18 years later in 1909.

Prince Rostislav is respectfully dedicated to 'My dear professor, Anton Stepanovich Arensky', as the latter had just agreed to let Rachmaninov take the normally forbidden step of sitting his composition finals a year early. His contemporary, Alexander Scriabin, asked for the same discretionary favour, but was so detested by Arensky that he was flatly turned down. Taking umbrage, Scriabin promptly left the composition class, and ultimately the Conservatory, without his composer's diploma.

Come January 1892, and Rachmaninov was once again at his most creatively mellifluous, composing in only four days his first *Trio élégiaque* for piano, violin and cello. Cast in one mournfully expressive movement, the piece seems never to have been intended for expansion into a full-scale work. In very much the same mould is the soulful song setting '*Oh stay, my love, forsake me not*', dedicated to Anna Lodizhenskaya, a married lady of gypsy extraction whom Rachmaninov had first met the previous year. His feelings for her bordered on dangerous obsession, although the true extent of their relationship has never been established.

Putting this disturbing emotional distraction behind him, Rachmaninov began to make furious preparations for the forthcoming premiere of the opening movement of his *First Piano Concerto*, due to take place at a student concert to be conducted by Vasily Safanov. Mikhail Bukinik recollected excitedly:

> *At the rehearsals, the eighteen-year-old Rachmaninov showed the same extraordinary composure that we were used to in more informal surroundings. Safanov, who usually conducted all the new student works, would alter anything he didn't care for, cleaning up the orchestration and removing whole passages if necessary. The fledgling composers, invariably overjoyed just at having their work performed ... did not dare contradict him, and would normally agree with all his suggestions without question. But Safanov met his match with Rachmaninov. This student not only categorically refused to change anything, but also had the audacity to stop Safanov in the middle of conducting, complaining of errors*

*in tempi and nuance. This was somewhat embarrassing for
Safanov, but he recognized the validity of Rachmaninov's need,
although a novice, to enforce his own interpretative ideas, and
smoothed over any possible awkwardness. In any case, Rachmaninov's composing ability was so obvious, and his quiet
confidence created such a general impression, that even the
normally dictatorial Safanov was forced to eat humble pie.*

Rachmaninov had one final commitment before leaving the Conservatory: the composition of a one-act opera to be completed in
every detail within a month. On 20 March, he and his fellow
students, Lev Conus and Nikita Morozov, set to work on *Aleko*,
an adaptation of Pushkin's poem, *The Gypsies*. This tale of revenge
centres around the gypsy, Aleko, who discovers his wife with her
lover and kills them both.

Remembering his infatuation with Lodizhenskaya, the gypsy
leanings of the work could hardly have been better suited to
Rachmaninov's mood at this time. Remarkably, he completed the
opera in just over three weeks, and after playing it through at the
official examination, was once again awarded the magic '5+'. To
Rachmaninov's astonishment, he also received the Great Gold
Medal and the discretionary title 'Free Artist', a high honour only
granted twice previously. Zverev, who was a member of the jury,
followed Rachmaninov outside, and presented him with his own
gold watch as a token of friendship. From then on, all differences
between the two were set aside. Zverev's watch remained with
Rachmaninov for the rest of his life, despite occasions when he
was forced to pawn it due to severe lack of funds.

No sooner had he secured a fairly lucrative contract with the
prestigious music publishers, Gutheil, than Rachmaninov once
again fell dangerously ill with the same recurring fever. Having
stared death in the face a second time, he composed what became
his most famous piece: the searingly intense *Prelude in C sharp minor*.
This was his first work to evoke in an unmistakable way the sound
of tolling bells, uncannily re-creating their earth-shattering resonances. The gloriously sombre prelude was given its premiere in
Moscow on 26 September as part of what Rachmaninov always
considered his professional debut. He later explained: 'One day
the prelude simply came and I wrote it down. It came with such
force that I could not shake it off, even though I tried to do so.'

The approaching end of another calendar year typically spurred Rachmaninov to compose, this time a pair of *Cello Pieces*, Op.2 (a mournful *Prelude* and languorous *Oriental Dance*), and then four companion pieces to go with the *C sharp minor Prelude*. This completed set was later published as the *Morceaux de fantaisie*, Op.3, and dedicated to Professor Arensky. Rachmaninov always maintained an uncharacteristic affection for these comparatively early offerings, although they lack the individuality of his best work so far. However, Tchaikovsky later told Siloti that he liked them a great deal, 'especially the Prelude and Mélodie'.

Rachmaninov now turned his attention to the forthcoming Bolshoi premiere of *Aleko*. Tchaikovsky was full of warm enthusiasm after attending the dress rehearsal, and following the actual performance roared his approval, excitedly joining in a general standing ovation to applaud the young composer's most notable public success to date. He even went so far as to ask Rachmaninov if he would mind having the work performed alongside his own recently completed opera, *Iolante*. Rachmaninov was astounded: 'He literally said – "Would you object?" – he was fifty-three, a famous composer – and I was only a twenty-year-old novice!'

Rachmaninov considered *Aleko* to be an inferior work, on later reflection: 'It is based on the old-fashioned Italian model which Russian composers have always tended to copy.'

Given the hurried circumstances under which it was composed, it is hardly surprising that the characterization is indeed less than three-dimensional. The ghosts of Tchaikovsky and Borodin haunt the proceedings from time to time, and there is very little sense of an evolving drama over the hour-long span, rather an attractive series of thirteen vignettes. Yet for a mere student, it is a work of considerable accomplishment and invention, skilfully orchestrated, and brimful of attractive ideas that consistently hold the listener's attention.

'I couldn't stay in Moscow . . . I was feeling quite depressed and just had to get away. So I did!' Rachmaninov informed Natalia Skalon in a letter of 5 June: 'I came here and began to get back to normal . . . I compose from 9 till 12. Then I practise for three hours. I am also very careful about my health: cold sponges, and four glasses of milk every day. . . . '

'Here' was the estate of the wealthy merchant, Ya Lysikov, at Kharkov. The glorious scenery and relaxed lifestyle away from the hurly-burly of Moscow inspired a flood of new compositions. Most were written in a small, pagoda-like wooden tower specially built for the composer by Lysikov in the grounds of his estate.

Rachmaninov began with three new songs, including '*Sing not to me, beautiful maiden*', a profoundly melancholic setting dedicated to Rachmaninov's future wife, Natalia Satina. These typically moody outpourings were then added to three existing settings to form the *Six Songs*, Op.4.

Work continued swiftly with the *Fantaisie-tableaux*, Op.5 for two pianos (popularly known as the *First Suite*), later dedicated to Tchaikovsky with his permission. Cast in four mesmerizing movements, it is one of the most prophetic of Rachmaninov's early opuses. The sound of bells is obsessively recalled throughout, particularly during the manic finale, which overflows with them. Rachmaninov's curious association of bells with weeping is made explicit by the third movement, 'Tears'. This was directly inspired by the awesome chimes of St Sofiya's Cathedral in Novgorod, which Rachmaninov had often visited with his grandmother. By comparison, the two short *Pieces for violin and piano*, Op.6 composed at about the same time (a soulful *Romance* and a gypsy-styled *Hungarian Dance*) are strikingly less personal in tone.

Rachmaninov's creative energies were fully engaged, however, by a new orchestral work, a symphonic fantasy entitled *The Crag* (or *The Rock*), Op.7. The title refers directly to the poem by Mikhail Lermontov, two lines of which appear in the flyleaf of Rachmaninov's original score, and also preface a Chekhov short story entitled *Along the Way*. Indeed, it was the short story that proved to be the real inspiration behind the work. Rachmaninov later revealed this by inscribing a copy of the finished score: 'To dear and highly esteemed Anton Pavlovich Chekhov, author of the story *Along the Way*, the plot of which . . . served as the basis for this composition.'

Along the Way tells of two travellers, a crusty old man and a gentle young woman, who meet on Christmas Eve at an inn. As a wailing blizzard blows outside, she is moved to tears by the story of his failed and lonely life. When she finally continues on her way, the old man is left standing outside alone, the falling snow covering the natural features all around him to take on the form of a beetling crag.

Given Rachmaninov's leaning towards the expression of the

darker side of human emotions, it is easy to imagine the appeal of this story. His moving realization of the woman's tears is tellingly derived from the third movement of the recent *Fantaisie-tableaux*, and he suggests with the utmost subtlety the sound of bells filtering through the snowstorm outside. Although perhaps not the most memorable or tuneful of Rachmaninov's early works, there is much in the general mood of *The Crag* that anticipates the dark foreboding of the *First Symphony*.

Rachmaninov's creative surge continued with his *Six Songs*, Op.8, all German and Ukrainian texts in translation, by the Russian poet, Alexei Pleshcheyev. The composer's natural melodic flair is well to the fore, generating a far wider emotional range than the general doom and gloom of the Op.4 *Songs*. Two gems are worthy of special mention: '*The Water Lily*', one of Rachmaninov's most alluring settings, and '*The Dream*' – a miniature masterpiece composed for Natalia Skalon.

This long summer of extraordinary productivity was later marred by the devastating news of Nikolai Zverev's death on 30 September. Rachmaninov's profound sense of loss was compounded the following month when Tchaikovsky also suddenly passed away at the age of fifty-three. Officially announced as the result of drinking unboiled water infected with cholera, his death is now more commonly held to have been suicide.

Rachmaninov immediately poured out his emotions in a second *Trio élégiaque*, Op.9, a three-movement work composed as a musical memorial to Tchaikovsky. On analysis, the various ideas within the trio have a tendency to sprawl, when compared with his recent piano concerto. The lengthy central theme and variations completely overshadows the relatively terse finale. However, despite this lack of balance between content and structure, the heartfelt intensity of the writing invariably carries the day, fully reflecting the composer's feverish devotion to his task: 'While composing it [the *Trio*], all my thoughts, feelings, energies were fully engaged. . . . I fought for every idea, sometimes crossing everything out and starting afresh. . . . '

Not only had Rachmaninov lost, in Tchaikovsky, a dear friend who had admired him since his student days, but also the composer whom he revered above all others. Rachmaninov was Tchaikovsky's own chosen successor, and one can only speculate what might have happened to change the young man's destiny had

Tchaikovsky lived a few more years and been able to conduct his disciple's music abroad. The immediate impact, however, was that, without Tchaikovsky's support, the Bolshoi promptly removed *Aleko* from their schedules.

The next three works were disappointing – Rachmaninov may have been laid low by creative exhaustion, or his mind may still have been numbed by the death of Tchaikovsky. Either way, his usually unmistakable imprint is much less in evidence in the set of seven *Morceaux de Salon*, Op.10, for piano solo with which he began the new year (1894), although this volume of diverting 'pleasantries' contains much that goes beyond the usual remit of drawing-room miniatures.

Rachmaninov was by now totally reliant on his income from composing and from the small amount of private teaching he could tolerate. His six *Piano Duets*, Op.11, were literally churned out, as he later confessed, to 'help balance the books'. He did not take them at all seriously, which may explain the lack of any dedication, and the fact that he never played them publicly – or even privately – to an audience. Unlike with the solo Op.10 *Morceaux*, Rachmaninov was keeping his sights firmly on the salon rather than the concert hall, resulting in what is in many ways the more satisfying set. Nothing, however, lessens the sheer banality of the *Slava* finale.

That same autumn, Rachmaninov put the finishing touches to a decidedly lacklustre response to such popular classics as Rimsky-Korsakov's *Capriccio espagnol* and Tchaikovsky's *Capriccio italien*. The *Caprice bohémien* (or *Capriccio on Gypsy Themes*), Op.12, topped off a string of unmemorable themes with a truly woeful cossack-dance finale and, according to Rachmaninov's biographer, Otto von Riesemann, was 'the only one of his children that the creator would prefer to disown.' It beggars belief that Rachmaninov's next major composition was none other than his *First Symphony*, Op.13 – a full-scale orchestral masterpiece in four turbulent movements.

Having spent most of 1895 on his magnum opus, he was forced to abandon it in order to go on a planned three-month tour with the Italian violinist, Teresina Tua – he had only agreed to take part as he desperately needed the cash. Things started out well enough, although Rachmaninov was far from impressed with Madame Tua. He reported in a letter that: 'She does not play particularly well; her technique is average. But she uses her eyes and captivating smile to extraordinary effect . . . and she is very mean with money.'

The mismatched duo reached Moscow during November, where Rachmaninov conducted the premiere of his *Caprice bohémien*, and then promptly informed Tua that, as he had not yet received a single rouble, he was resigning from the tour forthwith. This necessitated drastic action, and, not for the last time, Rachmaninov was forced to pawn Zverev's gold watch to raise much-needed funds.

Rachmaninov spent most of 1896 restlessly working on a number of projects while eagerly awaiting the premiere of his *First Symphony* the following year. Vocal music occupied a great deal of his attention, most notably the *Twelve Songs*, Op.14. This generally subdued set marks a return to the aching inconsolability of Op.4, and features piano 'accompaniments' of an often fearless virtuosity that threatens on occasion to take over completely. Yet among these songs exist a number of magical settings that have, inexplicably, remained in obscurity. These include '*The Island*', in which a heavenly vocal line floats over the simplest of accompaniments, and '*Spring Waters*', a life-enhancing song expressed as an almost unstoppable wave of joy.

Among the great 'unknowns' of Rachmaninov is a set of *Six Women's/Children's Choruses*, Op.15, inspired by the Maryinsky Ladies Academy where the composer was an occasional and less-than-willing teacher. Listening today to this sequence of highly attractive and emotionally engaging pieces, it seems scarcely believable that they had to wait until the composer's centenary in 1973 to receive their world premiere. More individual of expression are two movements of an intended string quartet, generally assumed to date from this period, his second and last attempt at such a work.

Rachmaninov's inimitable compositional voice is also heard to telling effect in the six *Moments musicaux*, Op.16, for solo piano, composed between October and December, which represent a huge advance on the Op.10 miniatures. Alternating violently between mournful introspection and explosive vitality, the pieces clearly point the way forward to the masterly Op.23 *Preludes*. Although the volatile *E flat minor Allegretto* (No.2) was Rachmaninov's personal favourite, it the quietly reflective *Andante cantabile in B minor* (No.3) that has proved the most enduringly popular.

Preparations were by now well under way for the premiere, on 15 March 1897, of the *First Symphony*, five days before Rachmaninov's twenty-fourth birthday. He travelled down to St Petersburg from Moscow especially to observe the preliminary rehearsals, which turned out to be something of a disaster. The main problem appears to have been the symphony's uncompromising musical idiom, combined with an almost macabre obsession throughout with Rachmaninov's musical spectre, the *Dies Irae*. It also compared rather unfavourably with the warm approachability of the old school's music as exemplified by Borodin, Balakirev and Rimsky-Korsakov, who 'did not find this music at all agreeable'. Glazunov, the conductor, was clearly not up to the task of handling a work so different in temperament to his own easygoing compositions. Having made a large cut in the Scherzo second movement, with Rachmaninov's consent he then tinkered with the orchestration in a number of places.

Rachmaninov, in trepidation, spent the entire premiere standing alone, just beyond the doors of the auditorium. The performance became a complete fiasco – Glazunov's incompetence was compounded by subsequent rumours that he had been drunk on the podium. As the cataclysmic final bars were hammered home, Rachmaninov fled from the building in a state of total bewilderment. The critics had a field day, especially César Cui, who gleefully stuck the knife in:

> *If there was a Conservatory in Hell, and one of its talented pupils was asked to compose a programmatic symphony based on the Seven Plagues of Egypt, if he were to write something resembling Mr. Rachmaninov's symphony he would surely have arrived at the perfect solution, and would no doubt thoroughly entertain all of Hell's creatures.*

Shortly after the premiere, Rachmaninov took off for his grandparents' house in Novgorod, in serious need of some emotional pampering from Madame Boutakova. As if in defiance, he began sketching a new symphony: it came to nothing. Having recovered from the initial shock, Rachmaninov appears to have been content to blame Glazunov for the complete and utter shambles. A letter to his friend, Alexander Zatayevich, is revealing:

> *I am not at all affected by its lack of success, nor am I disturbed by what I have read in the newspapers; but I am distraught and deeply depressed by the fact that my symphony, though I loved it very much and love it now, did not please me at all after its first rehearsal.*

Shortly before leaving Russia for good, Rachmaninov wrote a letter to his musical chronicler, Boris Asafyev, which pronounced more or less his final words on the affair:

> *It has some good things in it, but there is much that is uneven, immature, hysterical and bloated. The symphony was badly orchestrated and it received a performance to match. . . . After that symphony I composed nothing for about three years. I felt like a man after a severe stroke, who had lost the use of his head and hands. I won't show the symphony to anyone, and I'll insert a clause in my will forbidding its performance.*

However, this may not be the end of the matter. Rachmaninov's original manuscript for the symphony was headed by the striking biblical quotation, '"Vengeance is mine: I will repay", saith the Lord', alongside the dedication to 'A.L.' (Rachmaninov's beloved Anna Lodizhenskaya). Some see in this dedication a veiled reference to another Anna – Tolstoy's *Anna Karenina* – for the same quotation is used with considerable significance in the tragic novel. Rachmaninov shared the parallel predicament of being in love with a married woman.

It therefore seems more than likely that the failure of the *First Symphony* dealt the ultra-sensitive composer a crushing emotional blow that went far beyond purely musical concerns. The immediate outcome was a complete loss of creative facility that was to prevent him from composing anything of significance for another three years.

CHAPTER 3
THE BORN-AGAIN COMPOSER
(1897–1909)

- ♦ Creative recovery
- ♦ Second Piano Concerto
- ♦ Marriage to Natalia Satina
- ♦ Conducts the Bolshoi
- ♦ A break in Dresden
- ♦ Second Symphony and Third Concerto

Rachmaninov was utterly devastated by the recent symphonic catastrophe. So severe was his reaction that he suffered from neurasthenic pains in his back, legs and arms throughout the summer of 1897. His cousins, the three Skalon sisters, were on hand to see to his every need, although even they could do little to raise his spirits. His misery was compounded by having to complete a commissioned piano arrangement of another symphony. The composer? None other than Alexander Glazunov. Rachmaninov's aristocratic sense of duty helped him see the project through, despite his loathing both for Glazunov and a symphony that was, in many respects, inferior to his own.

Just as Rachmaninov's fortunes appeared to be at their lowest ebb, Savva Mamontov, the founder and director of his own Private Opera Company, stepped into the breach. On the advice of a mutual friend, he invited the composer to become Deputy Music Director for the forthcoming season. Rachmaninov gratefully accepted, thereby unwittingly joining forces with another conscript – the great bass singer Feyodor Chaliapin – who was destined to become one of his closest friends.

Rachmaninov might not have been so keen had he been aware of the reputation of his future boss – a decidedly mediocre Italian conductor named Eugene Esposito. The latter was understandably wary about the new appointment and the very strong possibility of being upstaged by the rising young star. Apparently out of spite, he gave the inexperienced Rachmaninov just one rehearsal to get Glinka's challenging opera, *A Life for the Tsar*, fit for public consumption. The orchestra responded well enough, but the singers were plainly all at sea, leaving the new conductor totally mystified. The problem was simply that he had not understood the need to cue the singers in. Esposito emerged heroically from the wings, just in time to 'save the situation'.

Rachmaninov duly reported to Ludmilla Skalon:

> *In our theatre truly chaos reigns. Nobody knows what is to happen the day after tomorrow, or tomorrow or even today. No one can sing – not because there are no singers, but because in our large company of thirty, roughly twenty-five should be dismissed for routine incompetence. There is nothing performable – the repertoire is large enough, but everything is produced so indifferently, so carelessly (with the honourable exception of [Mussorgsky's] Khovant-schina) that ninety-five per cent of the repertoire should be discarded or started again from scratch.*

Despite all this, Rachmaninov went on to conduct a highly successful first season. One newspaper thought he had already made his mark by the time of his first production, Saint-Saëns's *Samson et Delila*: 'His main achievement. . . is that he has transformed the sound of the Private Opera's orchestra beyond all recognition.' By the end of the season, the critics were almost unanimous in their praise, the final performance of Rimsky-Korsakov's *May Night* drawing an ecstatic notice from the *Russian Musical Gazette*:

> *He directs the orchestra a hundred times better than does Esposito. . . . If I were the manager, I would not even consider giving Russian operas to Esposito when they have such a brilliant musician as Rachmaninov to conduct them. . . .*

The magnetic stage presence for which Rachmaninov became famous is well illustrated by a memorable event that occurred during a concert tour with Chaliapin that autumn. Following one particular performance, the great playwright Anton Chekhov came backstage, and in a state of extreme agitation made straight for the composer: 'All this time I have been looking at you, young man. You have a wonderful face – you will become a great artist.'

Generous support from friends and relatives continued unabated. Most notably, cousin Alexander Siloti made a point of including the *C sharp minor Prelude* in all his foreign recitals. This indelible miniature created such a sensation in England that Rachmaninov was promptly invited by London's Royal Philharmonic Society to make a personal appearance. He accordingly made his British debut at the Queen's Hall on 19 April 1899, playing the *Prelude* and *Élégie* from the *Morceaux de fantaisie*, and conducting *The Crag*. The *Prelude* brought the audience cheering to its feet, although the *Monthly Musical Record* was less kindly disposed towards *The Crag*, concluding perhaps rather unnecessarily that: '. . . it would be unreasonable to suppose that all Russian composers would produce masterpieces like the "*Pathetic*" *Symphony*.' The *Musical Times* praised his conducting and playing, but was also less excited by the creative side of his genius. The Society invited Rachmaninov back for the next season to play his *First Piano Concerto*, but in accepting he promised to compose a new concerto specially for them.

Still hampered by his appalling lack of creative drive, Rachmaninov's anguished state of mind can hardly have improved with the news of Vera Skalon's wedding that autumn. They had corresponded, ever since their first encounter nearly a decade before – and while Rachmaninov's letters to Vera's sisters Natalia and Ludmilla have been seen to be perfectly open and friendly, there is every reason to believe that those to Vera were of a more intimate nature. We shall never know, as their entire correspondence was burnt by Vera shortly before her marriage.

It was the Satins, Rachmaninov's other cousins and 'second family' who finally came to the rescue. They suggested a course of treatment with Dr. Nikolai Dahl, a Moscow physician and expert in hypnosis. Remarkably, Dahl's mesmerizing repetition of certain key phrases ('You will write your concerto. It will be of superlative quality.') began to take effect less than a month into the sessions. Rachmaninov later recollected to his biographer, Otto von Riesemann:

> *Although it may seem ridiculous, this cure really did the trick. By the beginning of the summer I was composing again. Ideas came to me in the greatest profusion – more than I needed for the concerto.*

The Satins continued to do all they could to help enhance Rachmaninov's recovery – but this time the plan backfired. Through a family contact, they arranged a rendezvous with the great novelist Alexei Tolstoy, whom Rachmaninov deeply admired. The first time they met, the composer was decidedly on edge:

> *He invited me to sit next to him and stroked my knees. He could tell how nervous I was. And then, at table, he said to me, 'You must work. Do you think I am pleased with myself? Work. I must work every day,' and similar stereotyped phrases.*

Following this less than auspicious encounter, a second one was immediately scheduled, this time with Chaliapin in tow for moral support. The atmosphere was no less excitable, according to Chaliapin's reminiscences of the occasion. But the crunch came when Tolstoy invited Rachmaninov to play one of his own compositions:

> *... he was nervous and his hands were cold... I can't even remember what he played. I was too terrified by the thought that it would soon be my turn to sing. .... Then quite out of the blue, Leo Nikolayevich turned to Rachmaninov and asked, 'Tell me, is such music needed by anybody?'*

This was hardly the sort of comment designed to get Rachmaninov back into composing.

Despite this momentary setback, the composer was soon on the road to recovery. It was a long holiday in Italy that finally did the trick. Chaliapin had been invited to sing the title role in Arrigo Boito's opera *Mefistofele*, at La Scala, Milan, and had asked the composer to accompany him. Once he was settled in Varazze, a pleasant little resort near Genoa, Rachmaninov's creative floodgates burst open with renewed inspiration and vigour as he furiously set about making sketches for both his *Second Piano Suite*, Op.17, and most crucially, the *Second Piano Concerto*, Op.18. These were completed on his return to Russia, alongside the first of his remarkable series of solo piano transcriptions, the Minuet from Bizet's *L'Arlésienne* .

Rachmaninov capped this miraculous spate of creativity with his four-movement *Cello Sonata*, Op.19, his first piece of chamber music for eight years, and among the finest works for the instrument. It is hardly surprising, from a man destined to become one of the world's supreme pianists, that the keyboard part is a shade overpowering at times – yet the sheer quality of this enraptured music carries all before it. Indeed, it is hard to imagine how such a spontaneously exuberant and structurally assured piece could have come from the pen of a man who, just over a year before, was creatively impotent. Melodies almost fall over one another to be heard, particularly in the ravishing slow movement with its evocative mood of skin-tingling reflectiveness. Rachmaninov was back with a vengeance.

The *Second Concerto*, dedicated in heartfelt appreciation to Dr. Dahl, was premiered on 27 October, with Rachmaninov as soloist and the Moscow Philharmonic Society Orchestra, conducted by Siloti. Its success was instantaneous, although in recent years, the work's extreme popularity has tended to blunt its unique qualities. For audiences at the time, the opening chord sequence, suggestive of the slow tolling of bells, and the following dignified melody, sounding like some ancient chant unspiralling, touched the Russian soul to the core. Combined with the heavily nostalgic mood of all three movements, and the physical impact yet restrained virtuosity of the solo part, the potency of the concerto's emotional message proved irresistible.

Something that is less often remarked upon is this concerto's complete lack of affinity with the *First Symphony*. Rachmaninov would appear to have wanted not only to blot out the physical and mental anguish caused by the symphony's failure, but also its musical implications. The gypsyesque melodic and harmonic inflections and daemonic intensity of the symphony have no place here. Instead, developing upon the languorous style of some of his earlier piano pieces and songs, Rachmaninov forged a new creative path that set the standard for the remainder of his creative output.

Less than a month later, Rachmaninov and Siloti gave the premiere of the *Second Two-piano Suite*, another scintillating masterpiece that is only now, at last, receiving due recognition. The chant-like shape of many of the themes, the unmistakable evocation of the sound of bells throughout the whirlwind finale, and several concealed references to the *Dies Irae*, make this *the* Rachmaninov work *par excellence*. Lighter in general mood than both the concerto and the sonata, this suite brims over with a new-found melodic luxuriance and creative dynamism that irrepressibly combine to produce what is arguably the finest of all works for two pianos.

Rachmaninov began the new year (1902) in full creative flow with yet another masterwork, the cantata, *Spring*, Op.20, based on Nikolay Nekrasov's poem, *The Verdant Noise*. The story tells of a revengeful husband on the point of murdering his unfaithful wife, who suddenly holds back, transfixed by the first blossomings of spring. Scored for solo baritone, chorus and orchestra, this magical piece is largely neglected nowadays, due entirely to the large forces required for its mere fifteen-minute span. Rachmaninov's later doubts about the orchestration ('there is no sign of spring in the orchestra') were largely the result of criticism from Rimsky-Korsakov, who instinctively preferred brighter orchestral colours. Indeed, the ethereal final section is among the composer's most sublime utterances.

It was at about this time that Rachmaninov announced his engagement to his cousin, Natalia Satina. They had enjoyed plenty of contact over the years, and he was already effectively a member of her family. Yet the news still came as something of a surprise to their various relatives, who were only too aware of the extent of Rachmaninov's feelings for a number of other women, most notably Vera Skalon and Anna Lodizhchenskaya.

There were considerable difficulties to overcome, as Natalia was a first cousin and was therefore forbidden to marry Rachmaninov according to the teachings of the Russian Orthodox Church. Fortunately, an aunt came to the rescue and put the composer in touch with a willing priest who was then able to sort out most of the problems. Eventually, due largely to the family's military connections, the wedding took place in the makeshift chapel of Moscow's 6th Tavrichensky Regiment on 2 April 1902.

The next day, the newlyweds set off on their honeymoon, taking in Vienna, Venice, and Lucerne, where Rachmaninov composed his *Twelve Songs*, Op.21. He wrote, rather disparagingly, to

Nikita Morozov: 'I am keeping the songs by me for now: they were rushed off in haste, and are therefore in need of some refinement.'

Typically, despite these strictures, there is very little sign of 'haste' in these settings. It is notable, however, that the treatment of the darker texts, expressed in a style reminiscent of the 1890s, is less sympathetic than those that revel in Rachmaninov's alluring melodic warmth. Nevertheless, it was indisputably his finest collection to date, and included a particular favourite of the composer's, '*Lilacs*', one of only two songs he later transcribed for solo piano. The 3,000-rouble fee also helped to pay for the honeymoon, which came to a close with a gradual return to Russia via Bayreuth to see Wagner's operas *The Flying Dutchman*, *Parsifal*, and the *Ring* cycle. This was courtesy of the devoted Siloti, who had given the new couple the tickets as a wedding present.

The Rachmaninovs' first summer as man and wife was spent at Ivanovka – it was a radiantly happy time, marked by the composition of the solo piano *Variations on a Theme of Chopin*, Op.22. This remarkable work is based on Chopin's famous *C minor Prelude*, Op.28, No.20, and is ingeniously structured so that the contrasting characters of the individual variations create the impression of four continuous movements. Rarely heard in concert, the variations are less emotionally forthcoming than, say, the recent *Two-piano Suite*, yet patient listening reveals much careful thought, sensitivity and pianistic ingenuity. According to Natalia, Rachmaninov was particularly self-absorbed when working on the variations. He would often take to the tree-lined Red Avenue on the Ivanovka estate, and as each new musical idea occurred to him, would rush inside to play it through on the piano.

Returning to Moscow, Rachmaninov devoted himself to the composition of his first set of solo piano *Preludes*, Op.23, while awaiting the birth of his first child. A baby daughter, Irina, was born on May 14, in response to which Rachmaninov sat down the very same day and composed his *E flat major Prelude* (No.6), a microcosm of wide-eyed innocence and blissful contentment.

The newly-enlarged family travelled to Ivanovka for the summer, although much of the stay was plagued with illness, giving rise to particular concern for the new baby. Both Natalia and Irina were bed-ridden for a fortnight with sickness, and Rachmaninov fell ill with angina. Given Rachmaninov's almost pathological obsession with death since childhood, and the fact that he had himself lost a baby sister under very similar circumstances, this must have had a traumatic effect on the new father. It is surely no coincidence that the later preludes composed at this time are much less personal in tone, relying to an uncharacteristic extent on Chopin role models.

Once Irina was out of immediate danger, Rachmaninov began working on two operas more or less consecutively, *The Miserly Knight*, Op.24 and *Francesca da Rimini*, Op.25. This was a highly ambitious undertaking that would occupy his attention on and off for the following two years. Judging by the rather variable results, Rachmaninov had for once clearly bitten off more than he could chew.

The all-male *The Miserly Knight* (completed in June 1905) consists of three short scenes concerning a spendthrift baron who refuses his son, Albert, a share in his fortune. The central scene, lasting something over twenty minutes, is an extended monologue for the baron, who avariciously describes how he built up his immense wealth coin by coin. Albert then requests an audience with his father, bringing along the Duke of the realm for moral support. The baron lashes out, falsely accusing his son of plotting to murder him, and challenges him to a duel. Then, apparently overcome by his own callousness, the baron drops dead from a heart attack.

Due to the almost total lack of opportunity for ensemble work, Rachmaninov placed the emotional weight firmly on the orchestra, composing the vocal lines as a form of melodic recitative, curiously reminiscent of Mussorgsky. The effect is akin to someone turning the shape of his normal speech patterns into musical lines and was quite unlike anything Rachmaninov had attempted before. The long and sinister orchestral introduction entirely lacks the melodic luxuriance of his recent work, so that anyone expecting an operatic equivalent of, say, the *Second Concerto* will be sorely disappointed. Even the normally devoted Chaliapin, for whom the role of the Baron had been intended, felt that Pushkin's original was 'far more powerful'. This, hardly surprisingly, caused a temporary rift between the two chums. Nevertheless, Rachmaninov's old professor and mentor at the Conservatory, Sergei Taneyev, was extremely taken with the opera, noting that: '. . . it contains some very fine and noble music.' It was the critic Yuly Engel who best characterized the work's impact in the influential newspaper, *Russkiye Vedomosti*: '[It is] perhaps a *Kabinettstück* for those with the necessary refinement of taste to appreciate its exquisite quality.'

Francesca da Rimini turned out to be even more of a challenge, due in no small way to the decidedly economical libretto by Modeste (brother of composer, Pyotr) Tchaikovsky, which had been based on Dante's *Inferno*. Structured in the form of a prologue, two tableaux and an epilogue, the story tells of Lanciotto, who – correctly – suspects that his wife Francesca is more attracted to his tall and handsome brother Paolo. The latter attempts an intimate liaison with Francesca, who after trying to deny her true feelings, finally gives way. Lanciotto arrives on the scene, and in a fit of jealousy plunges a dagger through them both.

Given the relatively small amount of text Rachmaninov had to play with, it is hardly surprising that the orchestra is once again strongly featured throughout. In desperation, he had written at one point to Modeste urgently requesting some modifications, only to receive a few extra lines by return which he thought 'utterly banal'. Frustrated by this extraordinary lack of support from his librettist, Rachmaninov later reflected:

> ... there were simply not enough words. The second tableau and epilogue last just twenty-one minutes between them, which is totally insufficient. And the whole thing only plays for about an hour.

On a purely musical level, *Francesca* oozes atmosphere and is masterfully orchestrated. Yet the problems Rachmaninov experienced over the libretto are often all too discernible, resulting in a near-crippling lack of dramatic flow. The long, brooding orchestral Prelude tends to overbalance the rest of the work, and the high quality of both the Love Scene and Epilogue ironically accentuate the lack of first-rate inspiration elsewhere. Even as the opera went to press, Rachmaninov and Modeste Tchaikovsky were still arguing over the libretto. In the end, they came to a compromise whereby Modeste's version was printed in a separate booklet and then tacked onto Rachmaninov's final score.

Rachmaninov had by now reasserted his position as one of Russia's greatest living composers, and was also the capital's most sought-after conductor. The Bolshoi had recently invited him to direct a number of their latest operatic productions in Moscow, in addition to which he had already agreed to undertake an orchestral series for the wealthy musical entrepreneurs, Arkady and Mariya Kerzin.

Rachmaninov started his first (1904–5) Bolshoi season with Dargomizhsky's *Rusalka*. This created something of a stir, not only because of the marked improvements in production, but also because the composer had repositioned himself in relation to the players. He opted to stand in front of them (as is now traditional), when previously conductors had directed the chorus from the front of stage with their back to the orchestra. Yuli Engel gave the production his seal of approval in *Russkiye Vedomosti*:

> *There were new sets, new costumes, but most important was the talented new conductor with a fresh outlook, Mr Rachmaninov, who inspired everyone, from soloists to chorus and orchestra, to perform at their peak. . . . The sell-out audience clearly sensed this.*

With the opera season behind him, Rachmaninov turned his full attention to the Kerzin orchestral series, which included a performance of Tchaikovsky's *Fifth Symphony* that won rapturous praise from the critics. The composer Nikolai Medtner could hardly contain his enthusiasm. Having bemoaned the stifling effect of the indulgent changes in speed favoured by the great conductor Artur Nikisch, he reported excitedly that :

> *. . . under Rachmaninov, all this imitative tradition faded away, and we listened to the piece as if for the very first time; particularly astounding was the cataclysmic impetuosity of the finale. . . .*

He adopted a similar approach for Mozart's late *G minor Symphony*, which 'erupted, pulsating with life and energy'.

There were many reasons for Rachmaninov's extraordinary success as a conductor. He was a severe disciplinarian, expecting his own high standards from others. His acute ear was also capable of detecting the slightest imperfection in harmony, intonation, and balance – and woe betide anyone who made a mistake. Yet, despite his dictatorial approach during rehearsals, his conducted interpretations were invariably more flexible than those he gave when seated at the piano. He had a range of gestures that were all his own – not in the grand, sweeping manner – yet he communicated himself effortlessly, and had the personality to keep the players exactly where he wanted them.

Rachmaninov's second season at the Bolshoi included the premiere of Rimsky's new opera *Pan Voyevoda*, a work that did not exactly fire his enthusiasm: 'The music is poor, but the instrumentation is stupendous.' However, he obligingly invited Rimsky along to the dress rehearsal for comments. The latter was so overwhelmed by Rachmaninov's ability that he implored him to premiere his next opera, *The Invisible City of Kitezh*.

Until now, Rachmaninov had been largely untouched by political events. Despite the ups and downs of his own childhood, he still instinctively belonged to Russia's landed gentry. While he essentially sympathized with the cause of the working class, he had not the slightest intention of becoming directly involved. But he could no longer ignore the revolutionary fever that struck at the very heart of the Motherland's almost medieval political system. In January 1906, a peaceful demonstration mounted by workers outside the Winter Palace in St Petersburg was mown down by the militia, killing over five hundred men, women and children on a day known as 'Bloody Sunday'. Strikes followed throughout Russia, affecting every level of society including its musical institutions. Both the St Petersburg and Moscow Conservatories were eventually forced to close, and the members of the Bolshoi Opera and Ballet came out on strike.

Under such circumstances, Rachmaninov's new operas, premiered on 11 January 1906, could hardly have been expected to make much of an impact: and this was the case. The family left for Italy for a brief holiday away from all the turmoil, although any thoughts of composing were swiftly banished when Natalia and then little Irina (only two-and-a-half years old), became seriously unwell. Following her treatment from a Florentine specialist, the family decided to return home and head for the comparative safety of Ivanovka.

With everyone returned to full health, Rachmaninov was once again able to relax and enjoy the surrounding countryside. He settled down to compose a fresh set of *Fifteen Songs*, Op.26. The last of these, a setting of Rathaus's '*All Things Depart*', contains lines whose prophetic resonances are, given the recent political upheaval, strikingly apt:

All things must pass and there is no return to anything.
Life flies into the distance quicker than a moment.
Where are the sounds of the words we once heard?
Where is the light of the dawn which once lit our days?

Of the remaining settings, the most celebrated are the powerfully brooding '*The Heart's Secret* ', and '*Christ is risen*', a radiant outburst of uncontainable joy. Rachmaninov dismissed his Op.26 as 'mere trifles' – small wonder that his songs have been so woefully neglected when he himself so disparaged them.

Offers were now pouring in requesting Rachmaninov's services as pianist, composer, and particularly as conductor. The Kerzins wanted to secure him for another season, and the Bolshoi attempted to woo him with the Directorship. There was also the possibility of another series of orchestral concerts in Russia, as well as one in North America. Rachmaninov turned the lot down, deciding instead to go abroad, away from all the turmoil. In November 1906, the family left Russia, bound for Dresden.

Rachmaninov's arrival in the great German city was highlighted by a performance of Richard Strauss's opera *Salome*, conducted by the composer. It clearly made quite an impression: '. . . there were many things in the music that I liked, as long it didn't become too discordant. . . the orchestration is amazing.'

Rachmaninov had never made any secret of preferring texts of a tragic or sinister hue, so it is easy to imagine how the macabre goings-on in *Salome* appealed to his peculiar sensitivities. During his later years in America, he took Natalia to the movies to see the original *Frankenstein* – starring Boris Karloff – and was so overcome by the threatening atmosphere that he promptly fled the premises.

Considering the difficulties recently experienced with both *The Miserly Knight* and *Francesca da Rimini*, it is perhaps surprising that Rachmaninov's first Dresden project turned out to be another opera, this time based on *Monna Vanna*, a play by Maeterlinck. Everything went smoothly, yet having completed the first act and made sketches for a second, Rachmaninov abandoned work on it altogether. He later considered completing what he always maintained was one of his finest works, but subsequently discovered that the copyright was held by another composer.

Whatever Rachmaninov's reasons for leaving *Monna Vanna*

incomplete, there can be no denying the supreme quality of his next major undertaking, the *Second Symphony*, Op.27. The broad outline harks back to the symphony's fated predecessor in its ingenious use of an introductory motif from which most of the work's ideas are subsequently derived. Yet here the technique is used with infinite subtlety, far removed from the occasional sledgehammer approach of the *First*, helping the piece effortlessly to cohere over long stretches. Brilliantly orchestrated and ingeniously structured, each of the four movements can boast at least one of Rachmaninov's most ravishingly inspired melodies. Dedicated to Sergei Taneyev, the composer's old professor at the Moscow Conservatory, this supremely accomplished and richly imaginative work is now rightly regarded as one of the pillars of the Russian symphonic tradition.

Early performances of the symphony were given complete with all the repeats, a situation now reflected in a number of recent recordings. However, during the inter-war years in America, Rachmaninov agreed to a number of cuts, amounting to some three hundred bars in total, in order to get this potentially sixty-five-minute work performed. Some of his other works were later treated in much the same manner. Rachmaninov typically put on a brave face, apparently perfectly happy with these drastic alterations. Yet this seems to have been another smoke-screen, as shortly before his death he privately confessed to his favourite conductor, Eugene Ormandy: 'You don't know what cuts do to me. It is like cutting a piece out of my heart.'

Rachmaninov's preoccupation with extended structures continued with his *First Piano Sonata*, Op.28, a work that, at one point, he had considered turning into another symphony. The sonata was originally based on the Faust legend, the three movements bearing the titles '*Faust*', '*Gretchen*', and '*Mephistopheles and the flight to Brocken*'. However, these titles were withdrawn shortly before publication as Rachmaninov, typically, did not want to give too much away. This is an altogether tougher, more dramatic work, whose uncompromising severity of tone (at least in the outer movements) brings Beethoven to mind on several occasions. In place of the easy flow of the works that appeared around the turn of the century, the sonata's ideas are often of a brooding intensity, with material of extreme contrast being brought into uncomfortably close proximity. The emphasis appears to be less on the ideas themselves, rather on the way the composer handles them. Rachmaninov always harboured considerable doubts about this sonata, and, following his move to America in 1918, dropped it from his recital programmes altogether.

As a break away from all this intensive composing, during May 1907, Rachmaninov made his way to Paris at the invitation of the great Russian impresario Sergei Diaghilev. The latter had organized a series of five Russian concerts in the French capital, providing an ideal opportunity to meet up with some old acquaintances, including Rimsky-Korsakov, Scriabin, and even Glazunov. Two particular occurrences had an impact on the music he would be composing two years hence. Rachmaninov became friendly with the piano virtuoso Joseph Hofmann, to whom the *Third Piano Concerto* would be dedicated; he also saw a black and white reproduction of Böcklin's painting, *The Isle of the Dead*, which, having scorched itself on his memory, inspired his tone-poem of the same name.

Natalia, expecting their second child, had meanwhile made her way back to Ivanovka. Rachmaninov soon joined her there, convinced she was expecting a boy, but at 9.05am on 21 June, his second daughter, Tatyana, was born. There was little time to become properly acquainted with the new baby, as a European tour took him away during the latter part of the year. Understandably, he could hardly wait to get back and see Tatyana again. He sounds utterly dejected in a letter to Morozov from Warsaw: 'To tell you the truth, it's dreadfully boring here. I don't care what happens, so long as I get my money and leave here pretty soon.'

The *Second Symphony* was premiered in St Petersburg on 26 January 1908 to great acclaim, and was then performed in Moscow a week later. Yuli Engel reported:

> *Despite his thirty-four years he [Rachmaninov] is one of the most significant figures in the contemporary music world, a worthy successor to Tchaikovsky. . . . After listening with unflagging attention to its four movements, one notes with surprise that the hands of the watch have moved forward sixty-five minutes. This might be overlong for the general audience, but how fresh, how beautiful it is!*

The spring months were always a time of great joy for Rachmaninov, who loved to see the flowers and trees reawakening and bursting into blossom. Yet the will to compose seems to have eluded him during most of 1908, and he progressed no further than considering revising 'three pieces that frighten me: the *First Concerto*, the *Capriccio* and the *First Symphony*! How I should like to see all of these in a corrected, decent form!' In the event, only the concerto was recast.

The year for Rachmaninov continued mostly on tour, which therefore precluded any further thoughts of composing. The concerts were a great success. On 26 May, Rachmaninov played his *Second Concerto* at the Queen's Hall in London, under Serge Koussevitzsky. *The Times* reported enthusiastically:

> ... *the brilliant effect of the finale could hardly have been surpassed, and yet the freedom from extravagance of any kind was the most remarkable feature.*

Another highlight of the tour included taking the *Second Symphony* to Antwerp, which, despite a standing ovation, left the composer less than impressed:

> *The orchestra is large, and the attitude of the players is fine, but – the orchestra is very poor. Rather like the one in Warsaw, only even worse in tune.*

From Antwerp, he travelled to Berlin, for a performance of the second *Trio élégiaque* with members of the Czech Quartet, then back to Holland for more performances of the *Second Concerto*, this time under William Mengelberg. Artur Nikisch had meanwhile cancelled scheduled performances of the *Second Symphony*, and refused even to meet Rachmaninov as arranged, apparently piqued at not having received the work's dedication.

One particular recital this season assumed special significance, as Rachmaninov received the first of countless bunches of lilacs from an anonymous admirer who henceforth repeated the gesture at every one of his public appearances, both at home and abroad. This heart-warming but mysterious gesture was, of course, inspired by the Op.21 song '*Lilacs*', yet it was not until many years later, in 1918, that Rachmaninov found out who the admirer was. It turned out to be a middle-aged lady, Madame Fekla Rousseau, who only revealed her true identity because she became concerned about Rachmaninov's whereabouts following his departure from Russia.

The tour over, Rachmaninov returned to Dresden and furiously set to work on a new symphonic poem, *The Isle of the Dead*, Op.29, based on the Böcklin painting, the monochrome version of which had so inspired him in Paris a couple of years before:

> *I was not much moved by the colour of the painting. If I had seen the original first, I might not have composed my* Isle of the Dead. *I like the picture best in black and white.*

The painting focusses upon the cadaverous white figure of Charon rowing a body slowly across the River Styx to its final resting place. A small island towers above, the ominous rock-hewn depositories both sombre and insinuating. Rachmaninov's tone-poem is equally mesmerizing, its unusual 5/4 time signature producing music of extraordinary forward momentum, which uncannily suggests the oarsman's inexorable progress. The arrival at the island is marked by a climax of truly spine-chilling dimensions, after which the textures once more subside as Charon returns to his gruesome work. Even those who normally find Rachmaninov's music over-ripe, invariably make an exception with this hypnotically engrossing work.

Returning to Ivanovka for the summer months, Rachmaninov's thoughts now turned to the New World, which, though little he knew it then, was destined to become his musical base for the last twenty-five years of his life. He had been approached by Henry Wolfsohn, his agent in the US, to undertake a tour of North America, and in response had set to work on a new piano concerto with the express purpose of using it as his musical calling card during the visit. As always, Rachmaninov kept his new masterpiece firmly under wraps – even Natalia was kept completely in the dark.

Rachmaninov was not at all well during this time, complaining in a letter about feeling his fittest for only 'three hours each day'. The idea of the American tour also seems to have quickly lost its original appeal, especially as it had to be undertaken without Natalia and Irina at his side. His only real comfort was the thought that the profits would at least enable him to acquire a long-desired treasure – a motor car.

CHAPTER 4

FAREWELL TO RUSSIA
(1909–17)

- ♦ First American tour
- ♦ Ivanovka
- ♦ Correspondence with 'Re'
- ♦ The Bells and Vespers
- ♦ Nina Koshetz
- ♦ Escape from Russia

R achmaninov set sail for New York in October 1909, having only just completed his *Third Piano Concerto*, Op.30, in time for the voyage. He practised and memorized the staggeringly difficult solo part during the crossing – using a silent keyboard.

The whistle-stop tour started with a solo recital in Smith College, Northampton, consisting almost entirely of Rachmaninov's own pieces as he had no general performing repertoire at this time. Successful appearances in Boston and Baltimore followed, then a recital in New York, after which *The Times* uncharitably reported: 'Towards the end of the program many of the listeners began to feel as if they were prisoners bound for Siberia.'

Undeterred, Rachmaninov's hectic schedule continued, with a trip to Philadelphia to make his American conducting debut in an all-Russian programme that included his own *Second Symphony*. This time, the critics were unanimous in their praise. With barely time to catch breath, the composer sped back to New York to give the premiere of his *Third Concerto* on 28 November with the city's Symphony Orchestra conducted by Walter Damrosch.

Audiences immediately took to the new work, although the critics were generally less than happy, voicing reservations in particular regarding the work's 'excessive' length (roughly forty-three minutes). *The Sun* was coolly dismissive: 'Sound, reasonable music this, though not a great nor memorable production.' The *New York Herald* gave a more considered report:

> *The work grows in impressiveness upon acquaintance and will doubtless rank among the more interesting piano concertos of recent years, although its great length and extreme difficulties bar it from performances by any but pianists of exceptional powers. . . . Mr. Rachmaninov was recalled several times in the determined effort of the audience to make him play again, but he held up his hands with a gesture which meant that although he was willing, his fingers were not. So the audience laughed and let him retire.*

The *Third Concerto* represents a blazing climax in the style that Rachmaninov had been consistently developing since being mesmerized by Dr. Nikolai Dahl at the turn of the century. For many years it was overshadowed by the supreme popularity of its predecessor, yet it is now generally regarded as the finer work. From the gentle innocence of the extended, chant-like, opening theme, Rachmaninov builds a towering edifice of emotional logic, climaxing in one of the most exciting finales in the concerto repertoire. The composer's transformation of the main theme into the slow movement's wrong-footing 'waltz' is a stroke of creative genius, and the work's final section marks the high-water mark of the Rachmaninov 'big tune'.

The dedication went to Joseph Hofmann, the celebrated piano virtuoso, who, after voicing some slight reservations about the work's structure, never played it in public. The real reason behind this apparent indifference, however, is more likely to have been that Hofmann's hands were simply too small to cope with the typically huge spans required by the composer.

Meanwhile, the American tour continued successfully, distinguished by a second appearance in Boston where such was Rachmaninov's impact that he was promptly offered the Directorship of the Symphony Orchestra. He declined, finding it impossible to even contemplate leaving the Motherland at this time. In any case, despite all the public adulation, Rachmaninov was not particularly happy in America. He wrote to his cousin Zoya Pribitkova on 12 January 1910:

You know, in this accursed country, you're surrounded by nothing but Americans and their 'business', 'business' they are forever doing, clutching you from all sides and driving you on. Everyone is nice and kind to me, but I am horribly bored by the whole thing, and I feel that my character has been quite ruined here.

Four days later, he gave a legendary performance of the new concerto with the New York Philharmonic Orchestra under no less a figure than the Moravian composer/conductor Gustav Mahler. Rachmaninov was deeply impressed with the thoroughness of Mahler's preparation, and later recalled that when he came to rehearse the concerto, things were well behind time:

Mahler then announced that we would play the first movement again. I expected a riot to break out, or at the very least some signs of general unrest from the ranks; but the rehearsal continued as before. Indeed, the orchestra played the first movement with even greater concentration second time around.

This extraordinary musical partnership was tantalizingly cut short when Mahler died the following year, aged fifty-one.

Rachmaninov, who had been desperately homesick for much of the duration of the tour, lost no time in returning to Mother Russia. His improved mood at being back among his friends and family was short-lived, however, as he soon received news of the deaths of both the composer, Balakirev, and most poignantly, Vera Skalon. In response he composed the song '*It cannot be*', dedicated to Vera's memory, a deeply moving setting that was later to appear as part of his Op.34 set of songs, and including the bittersweet lines:

*When she sees me, she will understand
the meaning of my bitter tears . . .
But No! she lies . . . silent, still, unmoving.*

Rachmaninov returned to Ivanovka for the summer of 1910. This was a particularly special visit as he had now become the estate's official owner – the Satins could no longer cope with its upkeep. Over the next few years, Rachmaninov invested a large proportion of his earnings (as he later pointed out) 'in the land, in livestock, in machinery, mostly of American manufacture.'

Just how important Ivanovka was to Rachmaninov can be gauged from an unusually frank magazine interview he gave in 1931, having then been separated from the Homeland for over thirteen years:

> *Each Russian feels stronger ties with the soil than a man of any other nationality. . . . It comes from a kind of instinctive inclination towards quietude, tranquillity, admiration of nature where he dwells, and, perhaps, the quest of 'self-reserve' and solitude. It seems to me that every Russian is something of a hermit . . . I speak about those ties with the soil because I, myself, feel them very strongly. . . . Up to my sixth year I lived on the estates belonging to my mother, but when I was nine years old my parents lost all their possessions, the estates were sold and since that time I used to spend my vacations at the estate of one of my relatives, Mr Satin. From that age until I left Russia (is it for ever?) twenty-eight years of my life were spent there.*
>
> *In 1910 this estate became my own . . . it was called Ivanovka. To that place I was always attracted, whether to get complete rest and quietude, or to be able to concentrate myself on my work for which that quietude is very helpful. In all frankness, I must confess that up to the present, Ivanovka still draws me to it.*

This was an especially happy time for the composer, for he was able to indulge his passions for riding and fishing, as well as to plant some one-hundred-and-twenty willow trees, whose subsequent growth and development from mere saplings was a particular source of pleasure. Just as thoughts of death cast an almost hypnotic spell over Rachmaninov, so he was uniquely compelled and invigorated by the burgeoning of new life.

The summer was also marked by two major compositions, including his first extended sacred choral piece, the *Liturgy of St John Chrysostom*, Op.31, a neglected masterwork lasting in the region of one-and-a-half hours. Rachmaninov's devotion to his task was such that he even went as far as to learn how to read medieval Russian musical notation. In a letter to his friend Morozov, he excitedly reported:

I began work almost on the spur of the moment and then suddenly became absorbed by it. And then I finished it in next to no time. Not for ages (since composing Monna Vanna) have I written anything with such enjoyment.

The *Liturgy* consists of twenty anthems, some based on existing chants, others entirely of Rachmaninov's own invention. Although naturally quite different in style to the symphonies and concertos, the same intensity of vision is notable throughout. The composer put his heart and soul into a work that expresses his deep sense of communion with this ancient repertoire as none of his works had previously. Yet although he thought a great deal of it at the time, in later years he became rather dismissive about the *Liturgy*, viewing it as no more than a trial run for his *All-Night Vigil* (*Vespers*) of 1915.

The premiere of the *Liturgy* on 25 November 1910, was, according to one member of the congregation, a spellbinding occasion:

Rachmaninov came out on stage wearing a black frock coat instead of the customary tail coat. His tall, thin figure at the podium, and the sharp features of his face were particularly striking and beautiful; he embodied the mood of the whole concert and immediately transfixed the audience. Their solemn silence, intense concentration and inspired faces attested to the fact that Rachmaninov's music had found its way to their hearts.

The Holy Synod subsequently forbade the Liturgy's performance in church, finding the style too modern and overtly expressive, although concert performances in both Moscow and St Petersburg were unanimously acclaimed.

Rachmaninov's other major work of the summer was a new set of thirteen *Preludes*, Op.32. He wrote them at great speed in just two-and-a-half weeks, completing three of them in a single day. In referring to them dryly as 'little pieces', the composer couldn't resist one of his little moans, as always to be taken with a pinch of salt: 'I don't like this occupation and it's always difficult for me.'

In many ways the Op.32 *Preludes* are more individual than the earlier 1903 set. Each one illustrates a contrasting facet of

Rachmaninov's art, from the arresting call-to-arms of the opening Prelude, to the nostalgic flutterings of the popular No.12 in *G sharp minor*. A number of the Preludes betray the chant-like influence of the recent *Liturgy*, while according to the composer's pianist friend Benno Moseiwitsch, No.8 was inspired by another of Böcklin's paintings, *The Return*. Following the premiere, Rachmaninov never played them again complete, choosing instead to play selections from both sets of Preludes in concert. Combined with the *C sharp minor Prelude* and the Op.23 *Preludes*, they complete a cycle that are, between them, cast in every one of the twenty-four major and minor keys.

Rachmaninov's attention now turned to preparations for his first season at the helm of the Moscow Philharmonic, a post he had been offered soon after his return from America. Such was his success that by the end of his three spectacular seasons with the orchestra, he had established an undisputed reputation as Russia's foremost conductor. Great soloists of the period queued up to perform concertos alongside him, including cellist Pablo Casals, violinist Eugène Ysaÿe, and even Scriabin in his own *Piano Concerto*.

It is hard to overestimate just how important a part of Russian musical life Rachmaninov had now become. Not only was he widely recognized as a great conductor, but even in an age of great Russian piano virtuosi he was considered to be possibly the finest. In addition, with the arguable exception of Alexander Scriabin (whose later work was in any case hardly universally greeted), Rachmaninov was the Motherland's most respected and popular composer. Only with the meteoric rise of Igor Stravinsky and, a little later, Sergei Prokoviev, was Rachmaninov's supremacy seriously doubted, although, ironically, all three were no longer resident in their native country by this time.

Following a short European tour, the summer of 1911 was spent, as usual, at Ivanovka with the family, although Rachmaninov's letters of this period seem to indicate that the stress of running the estate was already beginning to take its toll. It was here that he began work in mid-August on his first set of nine *Etudes-tableaux*, Op.33, which by their very title suggest pictorial influences. Rachmaninov never openly confessed the various sources of these pieces, nor of the subsequent Op.39 set. Yet during the 1920s he sent the Italian composer Respighi details of five that the latter was planning to orchestrate. These rather fanciful descriptions have subsequently been brought into question, although they make for fascinating reading:

> *The first Etude in A minor [Op.39, No.2] represents the Sea and the Seagulls. The second Etude in A minor [Op.39, No.6] was inspired by the tale of Little Red Riding Hood and the Wolf. The third Etude in E flat major [Op.33, No.4] is a scene at a Fair. The fourth Etude in D major [Op.39, No.9] has a similar character, resembling an oriental march. The fifth Etude in C minor [Op.39, No.7] is a funeral march . . . the Initial theme is a march. The other theme represents the singing of a choir . . . a little further on . . . a fine rain is suggested, incessant and hopeless. This movement develops, culminating in . . . the chimes of a church.*

Further doubt is cast on the validity of the above by a later interview during which Rachmaninov asserted: 'I do not believe in the artist disclosing too much of his images. Let them paint for themselves what they most suggest.'

When compared to the extreme popularity of certain of the preludes, the études-tableaux have only recently come into their own. The reasons are not difficult to hear, for in place of the languor and melodic intensity of many of his earlier pieces, there is a new rhythmic pungency and harmonic angularity. Indeed, their unsettling changeability suggests an affinity with Rachmaninov's erstwhile fellow student Scriabin.

Complaining about the problems of writing on such a small scale, Rachmaninov despondently reflected:

> *. . . it presents many more problems than a symphony or concerto. . . . After all, to say what you have to say, and to say it briefly, lucidly and concisely is still the most challenging problem for the composer.*

Following the premiere, even the usually supportive critic Julius Engel felt that occasionally Rachmaninov had extended his ideas to a length that they could barely support. The composer's own uncertainty is reflected in the fact that the intended set of nine was whittled down to six shortly before publication.

Yet, qualitatively speaking, the études-tableaux are among Rachmaninov's most revelatory and uncompromising pieces. This first set opens, for example, with a restless *Allegro non troppo in F minor*; it presents a disturbing dichotomy between a spiky, goose-stepping accompaniment and a typically smooth, chant-like melody that is hammered home over the top. Similarly, the *Sixth, in E flat minor* – a whirlwind of half-lit, cascading semi-quavers, whose strange ambivalence shows a curious emotional kinship with Debussy's remote late style.

The new concert season started with an English tour during August which included the first London performance of the *Third Concerto* in the Queen's Hall, conducted by Wilhelm Mengelberg. *The Times* enthusiastically reported:

> *It is more than usually difficult to judge the actual value of this remarkable work from a first hearing, because it is almost impossible to disassociate the music from the extraordinary glamour cast upon it by the magical piano playing of the composer. . . . The climaxes are built with wonderful power, but the musical ideas from which they spring are also distinctive.*

Upon returning to Russia, Rachmaninov could hardly have failed to notice the increase in social unrest that had occurred during even his brief time away. The working classes were in uproar, and those in power were gradually losing their grip as the 'mad monk' Rasputin extended his mysterious hold over the Russian royal family and their immediate circle. Rachmaninov was also unwittingly dragged into a different kind of political conflict, as the media decided to focus its attention on his musical rivals. As a composer, he was constantly compared with Scriabin, and as a conductor, the rising young star, Serge Koussevitzky. The other men were notably more progressive in their ideas than Rachmaninov, the staunch traditionalist.

Of a more agreeable nature was the unexpected arrival of the first of many letters from a new female admirer, who merely signed herself 'Re'. It was only later that she revealed her identity as the twenty-three-year-old symbolist poet, Marietta Shaginyan. This set up a remarkable personal correspondence which was to last until just before Rachmaninov's departure from Russia in July 1917. His letters to 'Re' are unusually frank and open, suggesting that they represented an emotional safety valve for matters that he preferred to keep separate from his own family unit. Apparently the relationship remained purely platonic.

Within the month, just five days short of his thirty-ninth birthday on 20 March 1912, Rachmaninov was already calling upon Re's expertise in helping him select texts for a new set of songs:

> *The authors may be living or dead – it makes no difference! – but the things must be original, not translations and no more than 8 or 12 lines, at most 16. And another thing; the mood should be sad rather than gay. The light, happy colours do not come easily to me!*

By 29 March we learn from another letter that the books and suggestions had already arrived, and Rachmaninov makes a rare reference to his children Irina and Tatyana, then aged eight and four respectively: 'I love them terribly! They are the dearest things in my life! and the brightest!' Yet another, dated May 8, written in the peace and security of Ivanovka, shows how much Shaginyan's interest meant to Rachmaninov: '...I love your letters because every word in them breathes faith, hope and love: that balm to heal my wounds.' He also expresses his admiration for his contemporary Nikolai Medtner: 'I consider him the most gifted of all modern composers.'

Comfortably shielded at Ivanovka from the massive series of strikes that threatened to bring Russian society to its knees, Rachmaninov settled down to complete thirteen song settings, nearly half of which had been suggested by 'Re'. These were added to the existing '*Vocalise*', to form the *Fourteen Songs*, Op.34. This collection is generally considered to be Rachmaninov's finest, including as it does such classics of the genre as '*The Muse*'. This particular song carries a dedication to 'Re', the appropriateness of which is made abundantly clear by the closing lines:

> *The reed came to life with her divine breath, and my heart was filled with divine enchantment.*

Another favourite is '*The Poet*', a curiously unsettling and ambivalent setting, dedicated to Chaliapin.

Meanwhile, Rachmaninov had at last taken possession of his first motor car, 'Loreley'. After making a few adjustments, including fitting a new carburettor, he set about hurtling around the family estate at great speed, accompanied by his uniformed chauffeur just in case of problems.

Having confessed her real identity in a letter, 'Re' appears to have caught Rachmaninov in the middle of one of his characteristically subdued spells:

If I do not reply to your letters promptly, it is only because of the large amount of work I constantly have to plough through. I feel extremely tired and am at the end of my tether. At a concert yesterday, for the only time in my entire life, following one of the pauses I had a memory lapse and to the orchestra's great consternation tried for a long time to remember exactly what came next.

A family break in Europe centred on Rome helped to restore Rachmaninov's creative energies, especially as they stayed for a while in an apartment that had been one of Tchaikovsky's favourite composing haunts. Rachmaninov ambitiously began working on two large-scale pieces, his *Second Piano Sonata*, Op.36, and *The Bells*, Op.35, a choral symphony based on Balmont's translation of the poem by Edgar Allan Poe.

Illness once again intervened when both daughters went down with typhoid, resulting in a mad dash to Berlin for treatment. Both pulled through, although for several days Tatyana's condition was described as 'critical'. Back in the comparative safety of Ivanovka, Rachmaninov finished both works, although his greatest pride and joy was still 'Loreley'. He would drive her for hours, often visiting friends, many of whom lived a considerable distance away.

Come the autumn and Rachmaninov was again absent on tour, making eight appearances in England followed by a hectic thirty-six-concert schedule back in Russia. This included conducting the first performance of *The Bells* in St Petersburg on 30 November 1913, in addition to *The Isle of the Dead*, and Siloti playing the *Second Concerto*.

In the *Russian Musical Gazette* the critic Tyuneyev, was in raptures:

Sincerity and spontaneity have always been vital aspects of Rachmaninov's music . . . the barely concealed feelings of hopeless anguish and despair that first revealed themselves in The Isle of the Dead *are expressed with unusual clarity in* The Bells. *In Rachmaninov's new work are heard with special force the heightened anguish and noble tragedy characteristic of a great artist. . . .*

The Bells is dedicated to 'my friend William Mengelberg and his orchestra in Amsterdam', and scored for huge orchestral and choral forces, although they are handled with the greatest skill and sensitivity. Cast in four movements, the work portrays the human life cycle in terms of different kinds of bells. The works opens with a magical Allegro, the '*Silver Sleigh Bells*' (childhood), deftly scored and uncontainably exuberant. The '*Mellow Wedding Bells*' (early adolescence and marriage) is one of the composer's most glowingly contented slow movements, followed by a driving scherzo of inexorable power and forward surge entitled the '*Loud Alarum Bells*' (parenthood and maturity). The '*Mournful Iron Bells*' (old age and death) brings the work to a desperately gloomy conclusion, a conscious testimony to the last movement of Tchaikovsky's '*Pathétique*' Symphony.

A work like no other by Rachmaninov, *The Bells* moves above and beyond the achievements of the early 1900s, displaying a resourcefulness and exhilaration in his craft that is uniquely compelling. No wonder in later life he declared it to be his favourite of all his works.

Only a few day later, Rachmaninov gave the first Moscow performance of his three-movement *Second Piano Sonata*, a work that also contains several unmistakable references to the sounds of bells. The sonata was extremely well received, the press noting especially how the emotionalism of Rachmaninov's music was now tempered by a more obvious intellectual control.

Nevertheless, the problems associated with the use of material appropriate to large-scale structures for a solo instrument caused Rachmaninov endless problems, much as they had done with his *First Sonata*. The various ideas of the ferociously difficult *Second Sonata* almost collide into one another during the outer movements, a problem he sought to correct in 1931, when he published a thoroughly revised and much-curtailed second version. Ironically, this later attempt to tighten the structure resulted in the work now running like a series of edited highlights of the original. Rachmaninov went to the grave still dissatisfied with it, yet despite a certain lack of structural inevitability, the work brims over with glorious music, including a sensational melodic climax in the central slow movement, which must rate as one of the most sublime passages in his entire output.

Following an idyllic spring in and around Ivanovka, Rachmaninov took the family to a close relative's estate in the Urals, where he felt they would all be much safer away from the political mayhem that was concentrated on the major city centres. However, his strong sense of duty persuaded him to return to Moscow during the late summer. The gifted composer Anatoly Lyadov had recently died, and Rachmaninov had agreed to conduct a memorial concert on 25 October. This all-Lyadov affair included the latter's most popular orchestral work, the *Eight Russian Folksongs*, as well as several premieres.

Having composed little of any consequence during the whole of 1914, Rachmaninov began the new year in creative overdrive with his unaccompanied choral masterpiece, the *All-Night Vigil* or *Vespers*, Op.37. This inspired collection of fifteen canticles was written at white heat in less than two weeks, and dedicated to the memory of his friend and authority on medieval church music, Stepan Smolensky, who had died the previous year. The *Vespers* are designed to be sung during the night-long vigil in monasteries and on the eve of holidays in Russian Orthodox churches. According to strict Church protocol, it was largely based on existing plainchant, although Rachmaninov was allowed greater freedom in six numbers – he called them 'conscious counterfeits'. He later requested that one of these, his favourite *Fifth Canticle*, be played at his funeral – although in the event, it was not.

As with the *St John Liturgy*, there is little here that listeners would automatically associate with Rachmaninov's distinctive style. This mesmerizing sequence of unaccompanied canticles relies more on its cumulative effect than the impact of individual numbers. Yet when occasionally he does allow himself some expressive licence, as tantalisingly occurs towards the end of the *Fourth Canticle* ('*O joyful light of Heaven*'), the sense of emotional release is overwhelming. The *All-Night Vigil* has only recently gained recognition as a true masterpiece, one which gives the most vivid emotional potency to Rachmaninov's obsession with chant-like material.

Just as everything appeared to be going well again, tragedy struck twice: Scriabin died prematurely from acute poisoning aged only forty-three. Two months later on 6 June, Rachmaninov's old professor, Taneyev, also died – ironically, he had caught a chill attending Scriabin's funeral. Next to Zverev, Taneyev had made the largest single impact on Rachmaninov as a person, as is borne out by a memorial letter addressed by Rachmaninov to the Editor of the *Russkiye Vedomosti*:

> *He was our model in everything. . . . Through his personal ex-ample he taught us how to live, to work, and even how to speak, as he had his own inimitable 'Taneyev' way of speaking – concise, witty, and to the point. . . . He seemed to me to be the very personification of 'truth on Earth'. . . .*

Despite all the rivalry fuelled by the media, Rachmaninov combined with Koussevitzky to give a series of Scriabin memorial concerts, including the latter's *Piano Concerto*, and a solo recital that featured the *Fifth Sonata*. Radicalists in the audience were not at all keen on Rachmaninov's objective style of interpretation. Among them was the twenty-four-year-old Prokoviev, who went backstage afterwards to pass on his comments. He later remembered the end of their brief encounter:

> *In fairness, I concluded: 'Nonetheless, Sergei Vasilyevich, I think you played it very well.' Rachmaninov replied sourly: 'Did you think I would play it badly?' This ended our good relations.*

Early the following year, Rachmaninov made the acquaintance of another attractive lady admirer, the gifted twenty-year-old soprano Nina Koshetz. Having arranged through Siloti to give a series of concerts with her, he set about planning a new set of songs, specifically composed with her voice in mind. During a brief concert tour, he dropped in on Shaginyan, ostensibly to ask her to sort out some texts for the Koshetz songs. He was apparently quite inconsolable, his mind full of the fear of death following the recent double tragedy. He even persuaded Shaginyan's mother tell his fortune with cards as he desperately wanted to know how much longer he had to live.

Back at Ivanovka, a pain in Rachmaninov's right temple first made itself felt, one that defeated all attempts at diagnosis for several years to come. As a result, he headed for the Caucasus during May in order to take the 'cure' at the resort of Essentuki. In pain and creatively inactive, he was visited by Shaginyan with the poems he had requested. He was apparently in a fairly desperate state, totally exhausted, and constantly welling up with tears as he spoke, his voice often breaking with anguish. He talked of creative aridity, citing the *First Symphony* and how it had snuffed out his talent at a vital stage.

Rachmaninov did not begin serious work on the new songs until returning to Ivanovka for the summer, where he learned that his father had died from a heart attack just two days earlier. It seems unlikely that Rachmaninov would have felt any great remorse, as many of the problems associated with his early childhood can be directly attributed to his father. However, the sense of family and friends from his early years passing away one by one placed a colossal amount of emotional strain on Rachmaninov. Vasily was buried on the estate at Ivanovka.

The poems that 'Re' had suggested to Rachmaninov were more abstract in tone than the relatively traditional 'romances' that he was accustomed to setting. The resulting *Six Songs*, Op.38, are accordingly more succinctly expressed, more controlled in their emotionalism. The most popular setting is '*Daisies*', a mini-masterpiece that he later transcribed for solo piano.

The Moscow premiere of the songs was given on 24 October by Koshetz and Rachmaninov. Julius Engel recognized their unusually economical and direct style on first hearing:

> . . . *he did not merely emulate those composers who may be more instinctively drawn to modern poetry, but sought within his own unique style a totally independent evocation of this poetry.*

Rachmaninov had meanwhile completed a second set of *Etudes-tableaux*, Op.39, for solo piano. These are often of a wrist-crippling complexity, even by his exacting standards, as well as being considerably darker in tone than the first set. Eight are cast in the minor mode, and five of these make unmistakable references to the '*Dies Irae*' chant. As with the recent Op.38 *Songs*, the critics were welcoming, recognizing the new direction in Rachmaninov's style. The *Russian Musical Gazette* reported:

> *In the Etudes, Op.39, Rachmaninov appears in an entirely new light. The gentle lyricist has begun to employ a more severe, concentrated and introspective mode of expression ... some interesting developments have occurred in this fascinating creative voice.*

These were the last major works Rachmaninov would compose for nearly a decade. With the political situation looking increasingly bleak, on 7 January 1917 Rachmaninov made his final appearance as a conductor in Russia, suitably enough with a programme of his own works at the Bolshoi: *The Crag*, *The Isle of the Dead* and *The Bells*. He was destined not to conduct again before a live audience until December 1939 – in Philadelphia.

Meanwhile, rumours circulated about his relationship with Nina Koshetz, and both families were by now decidedly unhappy with the situation. It would appear that these slanders were unfounded, but for the sake of all concerned they agreed never to see each other again, at least socially. To save any further speculation, the Op.39 *Etudes-tableaux* were not dedicated to her as Rachmaninov had originally intended. Among the women who came into Rachmaninov's life at various stages of his career, Koshetz is the only one who appears to have posed a serious threat to the security of his marriage.

By now the political situation in Russia had become life-threatening. Rachmaninov, extremely disturbed by the turn of events, gave a recital in Moscow for the benefit of the casualties of war on the day the Tsar abdicated: 26 February 1917. This was to be his last solo recital in Russia. Another pair of army fundraising concerts saw him playing Tchaikovsky's *First Piano Concerto* under Koussevitzsky on 12 and 13 March, all proceeds going to casualties. On 25 March, shortly after his forty-fourth birthday, he played his *Second Concerto*, in addition to the Liszt and Tchaikovsky *First Concertos* at the Bolshoi, again for charity – few people in the audience would ever see Rachmaninov again.

Immediately following the Moscow concerts, Rachmaninov left his family in Moscow to go to Ivanovka, but by now no part of the country was untouched by the radical social and political events. The peasants were already in a state of unrest and he was advised to distance himself. He later recollected:

> *The impressions I received from my contact with the peasants, who felt themselves masters of the situation, were unpleasant. I should have preferred to have left Russia with friendlier memories.*

One of the older villagers, Anna Artiyomiva, vividly recalled his last visit:

> *The peasants of Ivanovka were already getting a bit out of hand: stealing the landowner's cattle at night, and raiding the stores. They'd often get drunk and run around the estate with flaming torches. They calmed down a bit when Rachmaninov came out onto the veranda, but he didn't say anything to them; he just shook his head and went back indoors. His music wasn't heard at all that spring; before, his music would have been heard night and day – but now Ivanovka was quite silent. Of course, in these conditions Rachmaninov found it quite impossible to work. He spent a whole month here in torment, then at last decided to go. He left Ivanovka for good this time and never came back. What happened to Ivanovka after his departure is very sad – the house was looted and later wiped off the face of the earth.'* [In 1973 work began on a full restoration, a project which is now well over halfway to completion.]

During May, Rachmaninov moved again to the comparatively peaceful surroundings of the spa at Essentuki, where Koshetz also happened to be staying. In letters dated 1 and 22 June, he expressed his concerns to Siloti, explaining how he had no money left, having invested most of it in Ivanovka, but that he had to get his family away from Russia. The ever-supportive Siloti tried to get hold of some exit visas, but even he could do nothing in the prevailing climate. Trapped in Russia, but pained by the direction of events, Rachmaninov briefly returned to Kislovodsk near Moscow to give a final concert with Nina Koshetz for the war effort on 28 July, where he also met the recently married Marietta Shaginyan ('Re') for the last time.

During August, Rachmaninov moved the family to the Caucasus where they spent the rest of the summer. He gave his last Russian concerto performance in Yalta on 5 September, playing the Liszt *Concerto No.1*. The following month, the Rachmaninovs moved back to Moscow, where, in order to get the worsening situation off his mind, the composer set about a long-planned thorough recomposition of his *First Concerto*. His very last Russian pieces, dated 14/15 November 1917 respectively, were a sixty-three-bar miniature entitled *Oriental Sketch*, later nicknamed 'The Orient Express' by Fritz Kreisler because of its hurtling momentum; *Fragments*, eventually published in the American magazine the *Etude* in 1919; and a *Prelude in D minor*, of a notably sinister tone.

By a stroke of extraordinarily good fortune, an invitation arrived out of the blue from Sweden to give some concerts in Stockholm. Rachmaninov gladly accepted. Swiftly he made his way to Petrograd (the revolutionary name for St Petersburg) for visas, was granted them on 20 December, managed to borrow some money from close friends, subsequently met up with Natalia, Irina and Tatyana, and with them boarded a train on 23 December, bound for the icy expanses of Sweden.

As the track terminated at the Finnish border, the family was forced to travel overnight by sledge along the road to Sweden, and then to join another train in the early hours of the morning. They arrived in Stockholm fatigued and bewildered. Their sole worldly goods were a few bits of hand luggage and 2,000 roubles. Some provisions, a thoughtful gift from Chaliapin, had seen them through the early part of the journey. The only music Rachmaninov had taken with him was the incomplete score of his opera *Monna Vanna*, along with the three new piano miniatures and Rimsky's opera *The Golden Cockerel*. He was destined to live in exile for the rest of his life.

CHAPTER 5
A CHANGE OF CAREER
(1917–27)

- ♦ *Arrival in North America*
- ♦ *Early touring*
- ♦ *First recordings*
- ♦ *Gershwin and jazz*
- ♦ *Failure of Fourth Concerto*

Wracked with fear and apprehension on being separated from the Motherland, the Rachmaninovs spent a desolate Christmas in Stockholm before journeying on to Copenhagen, where a friend had kindly offered them lodgings. Rachmaninov practised slavishly to prepare himself for the forthcoming Scandinavian tour, against which he had obtained a reasonable advance to see them through the first few harrowing weeks. By the end of the twelve-concert series, based on a staple diet of his own *Second*, and Liszt and Tchaikovsky's *First Piano Concertos*, the forty-four-year-old composer had earned enough money to pay off all his outstanding debts.

This still left the pressing problem of how Rachmaninov was going to support his family away from Russia. Composing simply wasn't an option. Rachmaninov was only too well aware that his existing music was considered old-fashioned in some circles, and he was not about to adopt a new set of stylistic clothing simply to satisfy the latest critical fads. He felt strongly that he would not be able to compose effectively away from the artistic comforting blanket of Ivanovka. It is hardly a coincidence that his few late masterpieces are mostly associated with places where he actively sought to re-create the ambience of his beloved Russian estate. He was also desperately out of practice as a conductor, and despite being offered the directorships of both the Cincinnati and Boston Symphony Orchestras, he could see no joy in spending the foreseeable future directing other people's music. That the world consequently lost one of its greatest conductors can hardly be held in doubt after hearing his uniquely electrifying recordings of his *The Isle of the Dead*, *Third Symphony* and *Vocalise* dating from the 1920s and '30s.

This left only the piano. After all, it was Rachmaninov's playing that had made such an overwhelming impression during his American tour back in 1909. In addition, the piano played a major role in the vast majority of his existing compositions. Rachmaninov could see no other way forward. He immediately set about a mid-life change of career from composer to concert pianist, spending the summer months frantically building a new repertoire, facilitated by his phenomenal musical memory.

Following a north European tour in the autumn, Rachmaninov collected the family together in Oslo. On 1 November they boarded a small vessel, the *Bergensfjord*, and set sail for New York. Although not all Rachmaninov's memories of North America were fond ones, it offered him the greatest chance of financial security given his near-celebrity status there. Following an arduous nine-day crossing, Rachmaninov arrived in America for the second time in his life on the eve of Armistice Day. Within hours there were celebrations everywhere. The composer informed inquisitive reporters: 'I have come to America to rest and work.'

Considering the bewildering change in circumstances Rachmaninov had endured over the previous few months, he was surprisingly level-headed and organized in his affairs. He lost no time in hiring Miss Dagmar Rybner, a talented musician and devoted admirer of his music, as his secretary. Her description of their first encounter in Rachmaninov's apartment illustrates the composer's eccentric shyness and awkwardness to a tee, as he apparently had to be called out from behind a dividing curtain by his wife simply to shake hands and say hello.

Friends and well-wishers also called to see what they could do to help out, including Joseph Hofmann, and the violinist Fritz Kreisler, marking the beginning of a friendship that would result in a small but remarkable series of recordings. Offers poured in from every conceivable musical walk of life, so much so that Rachmaninov hired Charles Ellis, his main contact at the Boston

Symphony Orchestra, to handle all his business matters. From the large range of pianos he was offered – invariably with lucrative financial incentives attached – he chose a magnificent Steinway grand.

Rachmaninov opened the 1918–19 season on 8 December in Providence, Rhode Island, his debut recital as an American resident. Little did he know that it marked the first of over one thousand appearances in North America alone during the next twenty-five years. He delighted audiences by marking each concert with his freshly-composed transcription of the '*Star-Spangled Banner*'. Although he never found time to commit it to paper, it had survived thanks to a piano-roll recording made during the 1920s.

Following a recital given in Boston on 15 December, a report by H.T. Parker appeared in the *Boston Transcript*:

> *Once embarked upon a performance ... he neither regards nor disregards his hearers; he merely bids them hear. With hands, with body he has not a trick of physical or technical display. There he sits, wholly absorbed in his task, entirely concentrated upon it, summoning, marshalling into it all that his faculties may give. ... The piece ends; with grave courtesy Mr Rachmaninov acknowledges the applause with which the audience yesterday heaped him: seeks neither to emphasize nor to prolong it; returns as quietly, as briefly, to the next item in the programme of the day. ... With grave goodwill he fulfils every obligation to his hearers – and vanishes.*

Rachmaninov closed his first season with three charity concerts, which included a sensational performance of his own *Cello Sonata* with Pablo Casals. During the remainder of his life, Rachmaninov raised untold sums for charity as well as giving away a substantial amount from his regular income to his relatives and loved ones who remained in the Motherland.

The American inventor of the gramophone, Thomas Edison, had meanwhile invited Rachmaninov to make his first records during April 1919. The composer had never worked in a recording studio before, and he and Edison argued furiously over which take was to be released commercially. In the event the records sold far better than expected, especially a performance of Liszt's *Second*

Hungarian Rhapsody, which included an astounding impromptu cadenza by Rachmaninov himself.

Rachmaninov was always meticulous about destroying pressings that he was not completely happy with. Yet despite this unquenchable desire for musical and technical perfection, he appeared surprisingly unconcerned about the sound quality of the recordings themselves. He found recording a fascinating learning process, but never felt that he could give entirely of himself in the studio, as he invariably did in concert. He later explained to his friends the Swans:

> *I get very nervous when I am making recording. . . . When the test records are being made, I know that they will be played back to me, and am generally more relaxed. But when it is time for the final take and I realise that this will remain forever, I get nervous and my hands grow tense.*

At about the same time, the Ampico Company also invited Rachmaninov to make his first piano rolls. Having enthusiastically endorsed the system, he went on to make thirty-five official 'recordings' between 1919 and 1933. The Ampico pianos ran on the same principle of a roll of punched paper operating a set of pneumatics that was already familiar from the less sophisticated player-pianos. However, the new system produced a far greater range of dynamics and phrasing, which made for far easier listening than the acoustic recordings of the time.

Despite encouraging sales, Edison failed to get back to Rachmaninov with a decent contract, and the Victor Company, seeing their chance, moved in and snapped him up in April 1920. The new agreement provided the composer with generous royalties advanced against sales, and a guaranteed minimum of twenty-five titles. Within days of signing, he was in the Victor studios recording pieces by Grieg, Beethoven, and Chopin. During the remainder of 1920 alone, Rachmaninov cut no less than twenty-six pieces onto disc, although due to his painfully high artistic standards, only five were eventually passed for commercial release. These new recordings still used the old acoustic method, whereby a number of horns picked up the sound and converted it into grooves on a negative master, from which the commercial release would ultimately be pressed.

Rachmaninov spent the summer of 1920 at the country town of Goshen, about two hours' drive from New York. Here he went for long drives as he once had in Russia, with just a mechanic along just in case of problems. Some years later he likened his love of driving to the exhilaration of conducting:

> *When I conduct, I experience much the same feeling as when I drive my car – an inner calm that gives me complete mastery of myself and of the forces, musical or mechanical, at my disposal.*

Apart from that, Rachmaninov was busy practising the first of the 'idea-programmes' which would become a regular feature of his solo recitals over the coming years. This first one was simply called 'études' (studies), with examples by Alkan, Chopin, Schumann, Liszt, Scriabin and, of course, Rachmaninov himself. The eponymous magazine, *The Étude*, wrote glowingly of him as 'America's new artist' and, in return, he gave them his 1917 solo piano piece, *Fragments*, as a publishing 'first'. Themes for future tours included 'ballades' (Chopin, Liszt and Grieg), and 'fantasy-sonatas' (Chopin's '*Funeral March*' *Sonata* and Beethoven's '*Appassionata*' *Sonata*). This set in motion a regular yearly pattern of concertizing and recording during the winter and spring, then spending the summer months relaxing and preparing for the next season's schedule.

The family moved into a house in Locust Point, New Jersey, for the summer of 1921, where a number of fellow Russian émigrés called in to see how he was settling down to life in the New World. Rachmaninov surprisingly failed his driving test at this time, apparently due to his continuing difficulties with both English and left-hand drive vehicles. Disappointed and frustrated, Rachmaninov was forced to engage the services of a Russian chauffeur.

Rachmaninov's main sources of recreation consisted of going out in a motor boat, swimming, and relaxing in the sun on a private beach. Meanwhile he had secured for the Satins, his wife's family, a safe passage out of Russia. They settled in Dresden, where Rachmaninov had composed his *Second Symphony* and *The Isle of the Dead* barely more than a decade before.

During these early years of touring America, Rachmaninov established himself as something of a popular phenomenon, and for a while was quite exhilarated by all the attention and acclaim. He could hardly complain about such perceptive notices as one in the 8 December edition of the *Boston Herald*:

> *Mr Rachmaninov's playing is distinguished by clarity. His dissection of a composition is not, however, pedagogic ... He is far from being a dry analyst, but he delights in exposing the structure of a work in an eloquent manner. In this he has no rival.*

It was not long, however, before the appeal began to wear off. In a letter written while on tour in 1922 to his new Russian secretary, Evgeny Somov, he vented his frustration: 'Five years ago, when I first started touring, I imagined that I might really enjoy this piano business; now I am convinced that this is no longer the case.'

Alongside his discomfort with the gruelling concert schedules came the inevitable frustration with his lack of creative output. One of the world's finest living composers, who might have been expected to produce two or three major works annually during his best years in Russia, had written nothing of any significance for over half a decade. On 15 April 1923, just two weeks after his fiftieth birthday, he wrote to his old friend Nikita Morozov:

> *... either from exhaustion or merely as a result of getting out of the habit ... I am not inspired to compose, or rarely inspired ... to begin something new seems to me unattainably difficult.*

One of the few things to have given Rachmaninov pleasure during this period was the opportunity to return to the European mainland. In 1922 he enjoyed a long stay in Dresden with his cousins and in-laws, the Satins, rebuilding relationships with family and friends. Of the many letters he received from Russia during this idyllic break, one stands out in particular. Writing from Kiev, the great piano virtuoso/composer Felix Blumenfeld informed Rachmaninov of a seventeen-year-old student who had just graduated playing Rachmaninov's *Third Concerto*, and was already playing the *Second Sonata* 'quite well'. His name? Vladimir Horowitz.

An extraordinary feature of Rachmaninov's early years in America was his mild flirtation with the latest popular music sensation: jazz. In March 1924, he was an enthusiastic member of the audience at the premiere of Gershwin's *Rhapsody in Blue*, played by the composer and Paul Whiteman's Band. Rachmaninov was so moved by this epoch-making event that in the middle of his next American tour, he stopped off in Providence to see the Band again:

> *... it expands and develops its material in an indelible and novel fashion which I find absolutely intriguing. . . . The arrangements of these pieces are a marvel to me.* 'By the Waters of the Minnetonka', *for example, is a beautiful theme developed in an ingenious manner that could not be improved upon.*

The most important event in Rachmaninov's personal life during this period was the marriage of his oldest daughter, Irina, to Prince Peter Volkonsky on 24 September 1924. But even this happy event was soon tinged with sadness, for, almost exactly a year later, the Prince died quite suddenly in Paris, shortly before the birth of Rachmaninov's first grandchild, Sofya. Given the desperate circumstances, Rachmaninov, who was staying there at the time, was reluctant to return to America at all. However, in an effort to ensure funds would be immediately forthcoming for his widowed daughter, he made plans to set up his own publishing house called 'TAIR', named after both daughters – TAtyana and IRina – who would then supervise the firm's day-to-day running.

Whether spurred on by his yearly contact with his beloved Dresden, or the fact that TAIR desperately needed some new material to get the company off the ground, during the winter of 1925–26 Rachmaninov began composing seriously for the first time in nearly ten years. Because of touring and recording commitments, sustained work was almost impossible in the United States, but the regular summer spell in Dresden finally saw the project through to completion. The result was no less than the *Fourth Piano Concerto*, Op.40, dedicated to Rachmaninov's composer friend Nikolai Medtner. In addition, he composed a small but valuable bonus in the form of the delightful *Three Russian Songs*, Op.41, for chorus and orchestra, dedicated to the great conductor Leopold Stokowski. These consist of '*Over the River*' (a long-time favourite of Rachmaninov's), '*Oh Vanka*' (a song Chaliapin had sung with the composer on innumerable occasions), and the so-called '*Powder and Paint*' song, another favourite, which he had also recently recorded with the Russian émigré soprano Nadezhda Plevitskaya.

Having completed the *Fourth Concerto*, he sent his hand-written score away as normal to be set by the publishers (TAIR), but was slightly taken aback by its physical size on its return. He joked with Medtner in a letter of 9th September: 'It will have to be performed like the "*Ring*" cycle [Wagner]: on several evenings in succession,' going on to say he was already considering making a few cuts, particularly in the last movement. His typical neuroses even led him to make a tenuous connection between the main theme of his slow movement and that of the opening movement of Schumann's *Piano Concerto*. Medtner, for his part, had nothing but praise for the new work, although even before the premiere, Rachmaninov made several further cuts.

On 18 March 1927, the *Fourth Concerto* and *Russian Songs* were both premiered by the Philadelphia Orchestra under Leopold Stokowski, with the composer at the piano. They were tolerably well received, although the New York premiere on 22 March was an entirely different matter. The critics discovered in the concerto a combination of sentimentality, monotony, loose structure, lack of originality – and overlength. A totally dismissive review by Pitts Sanborn in the *New York Telegram* summed it all up when he cruelly suggested: 'Mme. Chaminade [the Parisian miniaturist] might safely have perpetrated it on her third glass of vodka.'

The failure of the *Fourth Concerto* was perhaps not altogether surprising given that it had been many years since Rachmaninov's last attempt at large-scale composition. The fact that he had been busy cutting various passages since first receiving the score may have indeed shortened it, but paradoxically, the work had lost some of its original sense of flow in the process. Rachmaninov made several further drastic revisions including a large cut in the last movement, and a complete rewrite of the concerto's opening and its coda. The finale then lost a further forty bars as the result of the composer's final revisions in 1941.

Yet the same basic problem remains: whatever the quality of its ideas, the concerto simply does not cohere as effortlessly as its predecessors. As with the *Second Piano Sonata*, one receives the impression of a glorious kaleidoscope of ideas, rather than an organic whole.

Given the work's structural deficiencies, there is much in the *Fourth Concerto* that – far from suggesting a drying up of inspiration, as has often been suggested – points the way forward to the masterworks of the 1930s and '40s. Melodies are tauter, rhythms punchier, and both the orchestration and harmonic content has a greater sting in its tail. The finale possesses a manic, headlong quality that had been largely absent from Rachmaninov's music since the *First Symphony*. Yet the most memorable passage of all typically harks back to the lyrically impassioned music of the early 1900s, as towards the end of first movement, the violins climb way up with a heart-rending melody to melt even the sternest disposition. Typically, the rippling chord sequence outlined by the piano underneath outlines the *Dies Irae* in its lowest register.

Rachmaninov tried to put a brave face on the situation, appearing only too happy to endorse the criticisms heaped upon his new concerto. Yet its comprehensive critical failure hurt the composer deeply, opening up all the old emotional wounds inflicted by the public humiliation of his *First Symphony*. Rachmaninov once more fell into creative silence.

CHAPTER 6
A SWISS RHAPSODY
(1927–34)

♦ *Rachmaninov as pianist*
♦ *Kreisler and Horowitz*
♦ *Failure of the Corelli Variations*
♦ *'Villa Senar'*
♦ *'Paganini' Rhapsody*

Despite the wounding critical failure of the *Fourth Concerto*, Rachmaninov could at least console himself with the thought that in the ten years since leaving the Motherland, he had established himself as one of the world's most sought-after pianists. His nearly unrivalled keyboard agility was partly the result of having joints in his hands that were almost freakishly flexible. He could hold down a span of eight inches with the four fingers of his right hand, and then extend his thumb under, placing it four inches higher than his little finger. This must account for the phenomenal speed at which he covered the keyboard, as well as the fistfuls of notes in his own music that few other pianists could physically encompass.

Yet there was considerably more to a Rachmaninov recital than a heady display of pianistic virtuosity. Even before he had sat down, his hypnotic presence would have onlookers struck dumb. The great English pianist Cyril Smith once reflected: 'Such was the power of his personality that I have seen members of the audience cower down in their seats as his glance passed over them.'

When playing, Rachmaninov would sit almost bolt upright with his head slightly bent, free of all superfluous gestures, quite unlike the prevailing fashion of the times. Everything was made to appear effortless – his ability to sight-read even the most complicated pieces and commit them to memory in a matter of hours was naturally an enormous help. Even the most thunderous passages would be executed principally from the wrist and lower arm, hardly engaging the muscles of the back at all, resulting in a uniquely clear, yet pearly sound quality. He would retire as he emerged, with a shyness and humility that perhaps exerted the strangest fascination of all.

Rachmaninov felt that every piece had its own peculiar nerve centre around which the rest gravitated. It could be a certain change of chord, the climax of a melody; it might be loud or quiet, fast or slow. Yet if he failed to make this magic moment register properly, he felt that the rest of the work had become utter nonsense. He insisted that it was his own work on composition that gave him this special insight into the inner workings of the composer's mind. Indeed, each and every one of his own works possesses this focal point, some more obviously than others. Almost certainly, his struggles with the *Fourth Concerto* were largely due to a lack of this revelatory moment – or at least, in this writer's opinion, it simply arrives too soon.

Considering that Rachmaninov made a total of three hundred and fifty-five public concerto appearances, it is perhaps surprising that this part of his repertoire was so small. In addition to his own five works for piano and orchestra, these amounted only to Beethoven's *First*, Liszt's *First* and *Totentanz*, Tchaikovsky's *First* and the concertos of Scriabin and Schumann. The latter was among the very last works he ever committed to memory, specially for the 1941–42 season.

By contrast, Rachmaninov's solo repertoire was immense, approaching five-hundred different pieces, dominated by Chopin, Liszt, and of course, Rachmaninov. He recorded and passed something in the region of six hours of solo piano music for (RCA) Victor, including a number of remakes. This priceless archive, dominated by his own compositions, has assumed legendary status over the years, highlighted by such classics as Schumann's *Carnival*, Chopin's '*Funeral March*' *Sonata*, and the *Second Hungarian Rhapsody* of Liszt. Yet it hardly seems possible that out of the thirteen Beethoven sonatas in his repertoire, not a single one found its way onto black disc, any more than his renowned interpretations of Bach's *Italian Concerto*, Balakirev's *Islamey*, and

Schumann's *Kreisleriana*. Even more tantalizing are the various other recording projects that never came to fruition for a variety of reasons. These included the *Second Symphony*, *The Bells*, and *Symphonic Dances*, the complete songs with Nina Koshetz, and the two-piano music with Vladimir Horowitz.

Following a short break in Europe, Rachmaninov arrived back in the United States just in time to wish Horowitz well the day before his sensational American debut on 12 January 1928. The following month, in preparation for a performance of Rachmaninov's *Third Concerto*, the two met up again at Steinways piano hall to try the piece out. An admiring crowd quickly gathered outside, bringing the normally bustling New York traffic almost to a standstill. Rachmaninov apparently passed no comment about it at the time, but had clearly been impressed. He later dryly commented: 'He swallowed it whole.'

Another aspect of Rachmaninov's art that has fortunately been enshrined on disc is that of accompanist. During 1928 he made three recordings with the great Austrian violinist Fritz Kreisler; two in America (of works by Beethoven and Schubert) and a legendary performance of Grieg's *Third Violin Sonata* in Berlin. Two years later, Rachmaninov reflected on these particular sessions:

> *We recorded the six sides of the Grieg no fewer than five times each. From these thirty discs we selected the best versions, destroying the rest. . . . [Kreisler] is a great artist, but is not particularly interested in working too hard. The eternal optimist, he will invariably endorse the first set of proofs we make as wonderful, marvellous. But my natural inclination is to feel and then argue that they could be improved upon. So when we work together, Fritz and I, we are always fighting.*

For the 1928–29 season Rachmaninov began cutting back on his American schedule, to enable him to spend more time both touring and relaxing in Europe. He also became notably more outspoken in his opinions than his secretive nature had previously allowed. During a visit to Paris, he made some comments about radio listening which drew a decidedly hostile reaction from the press both in Europe and the Unites States. It was his opinion that:

Radio cannot really do justice to good music. That is why I refuse to play for it . . . it makes listening too comfortable. . . . Listening to music is much more demanding than that . . . you can't fully appreciate it merely by sitting with your feet up and letting it soak into your ears.

Rachmaninov subsequently never allowed himself to be recorded live, so that whenever he played as part of a broadcast concert, the microphones had to be switched off, and the radio station would play something else. Rumours abound regarding the possible existence of pirated recordings made at such times, but none have so far 'officially' come to light.

It was also at this time that Rachmaninov discovered a villa called 'Le Pavillon' in Clairfontaine, about an hour's drive from Paris. Here he tried to establish an Ivanovkian feeling of peace and prosperity. Like on the old Russian estate, there were pine woods where Rachmaninov loved to sit and watch the rabbits, commune with nature, and play tennis with visiting friends. Every day the house would fall silent after tea, and Rachmaninov would quietly run through a couple of pieces to keep his hands supple. After this, the house would return to normal.

Later, during this first of several stays at Le Pavillon, Rachmaninov learned that his mother had died. His only comfort following this tragic news was that the recurring pain in his temple had at last been eased by a Russian dentist working in Paris.

Rachmaninov suffered from aches and pains throughout his career, including acute lumbago which on occasion caused him to carry out his concert engagements in severe pain. In 1931, during a quiet moment at Le Pavillon, Rachmaninov took his close friend Alfred Swan to his practice room, and after playing for a while, the fifty-eight-year-old looked down at his hands:

The blood vessels on my fingertips have begun to burst: bruises are forming. I don't say much about it at home. But it can happen at any concert. Then I can't play with that spot for about two minutes; I have to strum some chords. It is probably old age. And yet take away from me these concerts and it will be the end of me.

It was his extraordinary single-mindedness and sense of duty that kept Rachmaninov going literally right to the end.

One particularly treasurable outcome of those summers at Le Pavillon was a series of short but invaluable home movies made by Chaliapin's artist son Fedya. They show the composer in the best of spirits, sat at the wheel of his car, playing pranks, and at one point even joining hands with family and friends to dance in the ring. It seems almost impossible to believe that someone of Rachmaninov's status, who died as recently as 1943, was captured on film on only this one occasion.

Reinvigorated by his discovery of Le Pavillon and the miraculous dental cure, Rachmaninov gave what was an unusually frank and revealing interview to the *Musical Times* while touring in England:

> ... *The older we get, the more we lose that divine self-confidence which is the treasure of youth, and the fewer are those moments when we believe that what we have done is good.... Nowadays it very rarely happens to feel sincerely satisfied with myself, to feel that what I do is really a success. Such occasions stick in the memory for a long time.... There is, however, a burden which age perhaps is lying on my shoulders. Heavier than any other, it was unknown to me in my youth. It is that I have no country. I had to leave the land where I was born, where I passed my youth, where I struggled and suffered all the sorrows of the young, and where I finally achieved success.... The whole world is open to me and success awaits me everywhere. Only one place is closed to me, and that is my own country – Russia.*

With his sixtieth birthday not so very far away, interest in the notoriously secretive Rachmaninov was at something of a high point. An old Dresden friend, Oskar von Riesemann, suggested a biographical portrait, and Rachmaninov agreed to meet him. Their first encounter was at Clairfontaine, where they discussed many things, although Riesemann never appeared to write anything down. The same relaxed approach was adopted at subsequent meetings and led to a certain amount of scepticism about the finished result. A letter from Rachmaninov to an old Russian acquaintance, Vladimir Wilshaw, concerning the final manuscript is curtly dismissive: ' ... it contains a great number of inaccuracies which prove that I could not possibly have dictated this book, but that Riesemann largely composed it.' It would seem that

Rachmaninov only passed the book for publication in 1936 out of sympathy, as Riesemann had recently suffered a severe heart attack and was perilously ill at the time.

At least one good thing did come out of the book, however, as after an earlier invitation from Riesemann to stay at his residence near Lake Lucerne, the Rachmaninovs were so impressed that they decided to make their home there. They bought some land overlooking the lake at Hertenstein, and then made the necessary arrangements for work to begin. Over the next four years, Rachmaninov watched over the building of his new villa with passionate interest. He even devised a name for it, 'Senar', from a touching amalgamation of their own names – SErgei and NAtalia Rachmaninov. He also acquired a four-cylinder speedboat, and developed a passion for chasing the lumbering pleasure boats up and down the lake.

It now seems ironic that, at the same time as Rachmaninov was busy fulfilling his dreams of creating a second Ivanovka in Switzerland, Mother Russia's less appealing side was rearing its ugly head. Rachmaninov had been persuaded to co-sign an open letter to the *New York Times*, dated 15 January 1931, which was highly critical of the Stalinist regime:

> *At no time, and in no country, has there ever existed a government responsible for so many cruelties, wholesale murders and common-law crimes in general as those perpetrated by the Bolsheviks. . . .*

Shortly afterwards, the Russian authorities seized their opportunity following a performance of *The Bells* at the Moscow Conservatory. The official newspaper, *Pravda*, pulled no punches: 'This music is by an emigrant, a violent enemy of Soviet Russia: Rachmaninov.' At the end of March, the situation was made official: Rachmaninov's music would no longer be studied or performed in Russia.

The summer at Le Pavillon was unusually productive that year. Most probably out of defiance at the recent drubbing-down he had received from the Russian authorities, Rachmaninov set to work on a new composition on the very day they arrived, 27 May. The *Variations on a Theme of Corelli*, Op.42, for solo piano, was completed only three weeks later, and dedicated to Fritz Kreisler, who had originally suggested the 'La Folia' theme, made popular by Corelli, on which the work is based. Rachmaninov was never totally satisfied with the piece, and despite its masterly overall design and moments of exquisite poetry, the feeling that somehow his heart was not really in the work is inescapable. Rachmaninov once wrote that above all music should 'exalt', something that, for all their subtlety and invention, the *Corelli Variations* never quite achieve.

Returning to the United States, Rachmaninov gave the premiere of the *Variations* on 12 October in Montreal as part of his opening concert of the 1931–32 season. The audience's reaction was decidedly lukewarm, as it later proved to be at several other venues. Just how despondent Rachmaninov had become over this profound lack of interest in his new work is evident from an extraordinary letter to Nikolai Medtner, written in the December:

> *I've played them* [the Variations] *about fifteen times, but of these performances only one was good. The others were slapdash – I can't even play my own compositions anymore! . . . I have yet to give one entirely complete performance. I was guided by the amount of coughing from the audience. Whenever the coughing increased I would leave out the following variation. When there was no coughing, I would play them in the right order. In one concert (I don't remember where – some small town) the coughing was so violent that I only bothered to play ten variations (out of twenty). The record number was in New York where I managed 18. However, I hope you will play through all of them – and won't 'cough'.*

At the end of the tour, only two days before boarding the *Europa* bound for London, Rachmaninov gave his opinion of some contemporary trends in music to a reporter for the *New York Times*:

> *For the most part, it gives nothing. Music should bring relief. It should rehabilitate minds and souls, and modern music does not do this. If we are to have great music, we must return to the fundamentals which made the music of the past great. Music cannot be just colour and rhythm; it must reveal the emotions of the heart.*

The summer of 1932 was marked by the marriage on May 8 of his youngest daughter Tatyana to Boris Conus, a family friend and the son of violinist Julius, to whom Rachmaninov had dedicated his Op.6 *Pieces*.

Meanwhile, the customary frustration at his lack of creativity began to show and his enthusiasm for the work on 'Senar' waned accordingly. He told Swan:

> *I've been very tired by these household cares. I should never have started it all. . . . How can I work? Even for my concerts I am working very little, and the season will start quite soon. Besides, my studio is not ready. I have no proper room to work in.*

Although Rachmaninov composed nothing this summer, he was greatly comforted by visits from Horowitz and the great violin virtuoso, Nathan Milstein, who both lived close by and dropped in occasionally to play duets and sonatas.

1933 was Rachmaninov's sixtieth birthday year, and everywhere he travelled he was greeted with constant media attention, resulting in a number of insights along the way. In England, he told Andrei Sedikh:

> *. . . somehow, since leaving Russia, I don't feel like composing. Change of air, perhaps. Forever travelling, working . . . I do not regret it, I love to play. I have a powerful craving for the concert platform. When there are no concerts to give, I rest poorly.*

And the *Daily Telegraph*:

> *When I was on my farm in Russia during the summers I had joy in my work. Certainly I still write music – but it does not mean the same to me now.*

From Brussels we learn that Rachmaninov's favourite work was still *The Bells*, and the reason for his neglect of the baton:

> *My arms have lost their flexibility, and handling the baton requires an energy that I must conserve for my recitals. . . .*

Also that the only modern work he played was Poulenc's *Toccata*:

> *This is distinguished by spontaneous inspiration, and it is written*
> *for a musician of temperament.*

Perhaps his greatest pleasure of all was in the news that his music was being played in Russia again, if only as a political tool to show such 'revolutionaries' as Shostakovich what 'Soviet' music should really sound like.

The following European season included a celebrated recital on 10 March 1934, after which he informed the *Monthly Musical Record*:

> *I am aware that my playing varies from day to day. A pianist*
> *is the slave of acoustics. Only when I have played my very first*
> *item, tested the acoustics of the hall, and felt the general atmos-*
> *phere, do I know in what mood I shall find myself at a recital.*
> *In a way this is unsatisfactory for me, but, artistically, it is*
> *perhaps a better thing never to be certain what one will do than*
> *to attain an unvarying level of performance that may easily*
> *develop into mere mechanical routine.*

The most exciting news that year was the that 'Villa Senar' was finally completed, and furthermore that Steinways had delivered a concert grand piano as the ideal house-warming present. Arriving at Senar at the beginning of July, he immediately launched into work on his *Rhapsody on a Theme of Paganini*, Op.43, for piano and orchestra. This is based on Paganini's famous solo violin *Caprice in A minor*, itself a set of variations, and the subject of treatments by composers as varied as Brahms and Andrew Lloyd-Webber. As always, no one else knew quite what was going on until 18 August, when Rachmaninov emerged triumphant from Senar's music room, having completed what many consider to be his finest work.

Rachmaninov treats Paganini's famous theme to a glittering array of pianistic intricacy and orchestral wizardry, underpinning the entire work by a number of references to the *Dies Irae*. This is first announced by the piano in Variation VII, and finally rings out triumphantly just before the work's concluding flourish, capped by the composer's impish, throwaway ending. But perhaps the most ingenious invention of all lies hidden in Variation XVIII. Although sounding for all the world as though it were merely another of Rachmaninov's inimitable, spiralling melodies, closer inspection reveals that this glorious tune is simply the original theme with all its intervals turned upside down.

The new American tour started on 3 October, highlighted by the premiere of the *Paganini Rhapsody* on 7 November in Baltimore with the Philadelphia Orchestra under Stokowski. It scored an immediate success, and for once even the critics were unanimous in their praise. Only a month-and-a-half later, during a break in the continuing American tour, the same artists were ushered into the studio by RCA, for a remarkable recording made in a single day on Christmas Eve that remains the yardstick by which all other recorded versions are measured.

A highlight of the year's customary European tour was a London performance of the *Paganini Rhapsody* under Sir Thomas Beecham. Rachmaninov was clearly delighted and exhilarated by the reception. However, in an interview for the *Monthly Musical Record*, his lingering doubts and typical lack of self-confidence bubble to the surface:

> ... *perhaps I feel that the kind of music I care to write is not acceptable today ... for when I left Russia, I left behind me the desire to compose: losing my country, I lost myself also. To the exile whose musical roots, traditions and background have been annihilated, there remains no desire for self-expression.*

Rachmaninov's daughters were at Senar that summer, along with their children – Irina's Sofya, now nine, and Tatyana's two-year-old son Alexander. Following the scorching success of the *Rhapsody*, Rachmaninov was on the crest of a new wave of creative optimism and confidence, and was already turning over ideas in his mind for a new symphony.

CHAPTER 7
THE FINAL CURTAIN
(1935–43)

- ♦ *Third Symphony*
- ♦ *Escape from Europe*
- ♦ *Symphonic Dances*
- ♦ *Final tour*

Rachmaninov's second summer at Senar was devoted to extensive work on his *Third Symphony*, Op.44. The first movement was composed at a fairly leisurely pace between June and August, followed swiftly by the second only a month later. The finale unfortunately had to be shelved due to the impending start of a new concert season: 'I must give it up and sit down at the piano, which I haven't been very diligent about lately.'

Back in the US, Rachmaninov found himself regularly hailed with the kind of cult admiration normally reserved for film stars. A performance of the *Rhapsody* in Chicago during October was greeted so warmly that he was forced to repeat the second half. Further performances, in Minneapolis under Ormandy and Philadelphia under Stokowski, were greeted with standing ovations. Such was the extraordinary public demand to hear the new work that an extra New York performance, also conducted by Stokowski, was tagged on to the end of the original schedule.

The rejuvenated Rachmaninov made his usual return Atlantic crossing only to discover that Hitler's marauding armies had reoccupied the Rhineland, throwing down the gauntlet to the rest of Europe. Greatly troubled by the news, he made his way back to Villa Senar.

The early part of the summer was marred by an incident on the lake which very nearly ended in disaster. A potential tragedy was averted by Rachmaninov's last-minute intervention at the wheel when a friend lost control and nearly capsized his speed-boat. Fully recovered, during June 1935 he composed the third movement finale of the new symphony and then drove with his wife to Aix-les-Bains to receive some treatment on the little finger of his right hand, which was slightly swollen and proving increasingly painful to play with. They stayed at the sanatorium for over a month.

Rachmaninov was back in England during October. The usual hectic round of engagements was highlighted by sensational performances of the *Paganini Rhapsody* in London, and *The Bells* in Sheffield, for which he had specifically revised the third movement's choral parts. Both were directed by Henry Wood, founder of the famous London Promenade Concerts.

Rachmaninov returned to the US just in time to witness final preparations for the premiere of his *Third Symphony* on 6 November 1936 by the Philadelphia Orchestra, conducted by Stokowski. Reactions were somewhat muted – Edwin Schloss in the *Philadelphia Record* went so far as to describe it as 'a disappointment'. Subsequent performances in St Louis, Pittsburgh and Chicago under different conductors proved no more successful. The Philadelphia Orchestra then went on tour with Rachmaninov and Eugene Ormandy, their new associate conductor, taking in New York, Philadelphia, Washington and Baltimore, during which the new symphony was played on several occasions, but simply failed to excite either public or critics. Olin Downes in the *New York Times* summed up the prevailing mood: 'Would not a pair of shears benefit the proportions of the work?'

Rachmaninov, who believed deeply in the symphony, was wounded by its comparative failure. Such relative concision – the telescoping of the scherzo into the central section of the slow movement, the conservatism of harmonic language and increased transparency of orchestration – took audiences by surprise. The work's distinct 'Russianness' was missed by westerners, but it was popularly dubbed the '*Russian*' *Symphony* when it was premiered in Russia on 11 July 1943, shortly after the composer's death. The *Third Symphony* is now recognized as the last great utterance of the Russian Romantic symphonic tradition, in which the economy of means employed actually intensifies the extraordinary emotional potency of Rachmaninov's unique sound-world.

The 1937–38 season, which included thirty-four concerts in America, was scheduled to climax in Vienna, where Rachmaninov was to conduct *The Bells* and the *Third Symphony*. He got as far as the Austrian capital only to find it gripped by an outbreak of uncontrollable political fever. He managed very little sleep that night due to the constant chanting of the crowds outside, calling out the name of their new saviour: Adolf Hitler. All concerts in the city were cancelled just three days before he was due to conduct. Things went from bad to worse when shortly after the Viennese fiasco, Rachmaninov heard the news that Chaliapin was seriously ill. He visited him every day until his death on 11 April 1938. The composer was utterly devastated by the loss.

Over the years, Rachmaninov had developed a very special relationship with British audiences. This mutual bond was strengthened when, during the following August, an all-Rachmaninov 'Prom' was given, which included the *Third Symphony*. To Rachmaninov's uncontainable joy, the audience immediately took the work to their hearts, giving it the standing ovation he had so desperately sought in America. Rachmaninov was back in London for Sir Henry Wood's Jubilee concert on 5 October to play his *Second Concerto*, the only foreign musician so honoured. He stayed on for the second half, which included the premiere of Vaughan Williams's glorious *Serenade to Music*. The sixty-five-year-old Rachmaninov sat at the back of his box weeping openly.

At an age when most people would be seriously considering retirement, the very next day Rachmaninov was on a liner heading back to the United States for the latest round of thirty-nine concerts. During the tour, Alfred Frankenstein in the *San Francisco Chronicle* summed up his position at this time as well as anyone:

> *Today, Sergei Rachmaninov stands at the pinnacle of his gigantic career. His recital last night at the Opera House demonstrated that we are privileged to witness a kind of pianistic kingship that in future years will be enshrined in the mythology of music as one of the colossal and incredible achievements of the old great times, much as the performances of Liszt are now regarded. For Rachmaninov, despite his pessimism regarding the present state of music and his almost total reliance on the literature of the past, is one of the four or five very great lords of the interpretative realm, so far as the piano is concerned. He has held that position*

> *for long, but, if the recollection of past recitals can be relied on, his*
> *art has ripened even further and more gloriously in recent years.*

Rachmaninov's customary break at Senar was marred during the spring of 1939 by an awkward fall at home, after which he could do little more than hobble around the house with the use of a cane. We learn from a letter to Somov of his increasing concern about the advancing German armies:

> *We live as before – that is, not very calmly. Evidently calm has*
> *departed from those who live in Europe, even though war does*
> *not come . . . I've tied myself to a festival in Lucerne. . . . To be the*
> *first to run away seems improper in every way. But after the 11th*
> *[August] I shall consider myself justified in displaying weakness.*
> *Perhaps we can then leave, or rather, take to our heels . . . I just*
> *broke off this letter to glance at the local afternoon paper. News*
> *is again worse! So it goes from day to day. That there should be*
> *such possibilities in the world! Unthinkable!*

Rachmaninov also gave some extremely frank insights into his attitude to modern music to Leonard Liebling of *The Musical Courier*. So personal were they that he forbade them to be published until after his death:

> *I feel like a ghost wandering in a world grown alien. I cannot*
> *cast out the old way of writing, and I cannot acquire the new. I*
> *have made intense efforts to feel the musical manner of today,*
> *but it will not come to me . . . I always feel that my own music*
> *and my reactions to all music remained spiritually the same,*
> *unendingly obedient in trying to create beauty . . . the new kind*
> *of music seems to come not from the heart but from the head. Its*
> *composers think rather than feel. They have not the capacity to*
> *make their works 'exalt' . . . they meditate, protest, analyze, rea-*
> *son, calculate, and brood – but they do not exalt.*

With the German threat to Europe ominously gaining momentum, Rachmaninov was forced to concede that he might never see 'Senar' again. He went through with a planned concert at the Lucerne Festival, playing Beethoven's *First Concerto* and the *Paganini Rhapsody*, conducted by Ernest Ansermet. This turned out

to be Rachmaninov's last public appearance in Europe. Rachmaninov and Natalia travelled swiftly to Paris, and having resigned
themselves to the inevitability of war, on 23 August set sail from
Cherbourg on the *Aquitania* bound for the comparative safety of
New York. They were accompanied by Irina and Sofya, although
Tatyana opted to stay behind with her husband Boris, and their
son Alexander. To ease their anxiety, Rachmaninov bought them
a little estate about forty miles outside Paris – this was the last
time he would ever see his youngest daughter and six-year-old
grandson.

The 1939–40 season was something of a personal triumph.
Rachmaninov was conducting in public for the first time since
1910, in a demanding programme: his *Third Symphony* and *The
Bells*, both of which had previously been coolly received in the
United States. The audience was ecstatic. RCA, realizing that
Rachmaninov was still a commercially viable property, promptly
moved in and recorded the *Third Symphony*. They followed this
up with a coupling of the *First* and *Third Concertos*, mostly recorded
in a single day. Rachmaninov was apparently rather tetchy, and
found it difficult to tolerate the many distractions in the studio.
Indeed, at one point when the red light came on to start a take,
he frustratedly banged the piano in protest. The light was henceforth placed well out of Rachmaninov's line of vision.

For the summer, Rachmaninov rented a magnificent house
at Orchard Point on Long Island, set in seventeen secluded acres.
Another of the composer's 'pseudo-Ivanovkas', it even had its
own pier where he moored his new cabin-cruiser – the *Senar*. The
only blight on the summer was the news that during June 1940,
Hitler's armies of occupation had taken France. As communica-
tions were becoming increasingly difficult, they were unable to
get news of Tatyana and her family.

Rachmaninov then amazed his friends and family by settling
down to compose what would turn out to be his last major work,
the *Symphonic Dances*, Op.45, dedicated to Eugene Ormandy and
the Philadelphia Orchestra. He wrote it initially for two pianos,
from which he then made a full orchestral score. On 21 August
1940, he wrote to Ormandy:

> *Last week I finished a new symphonic piece, which I naturally
> want to give first to you and your orchestra. It is called* Fantastic

Dances . . . *I should be very glad if, upon your return, you would drop over to our place. I should like to play the piece for you. . . .*

Rachmaninov originally planned to call the three movements 'Noon', 'Twilight' and 'Midnight', but as with the *First Sonata* later withdrew them before publication so as not to give too much away.

The premiere was given by the dedicatees in Philadelphia on 3 January 1941. Critical reaction was characteristically indifferent, although the audience were ecstatic in their appreciation, calling him up onto the stage to take a bow. New York did not take quite so kindly to it. The *World-Telegram* scoffed: 'The work is long, derivative . . . and sounds like a rehash of old tricks – and the performance did nothing to rescue it from itself.'

The combination of uncompromising march rhythms and heavy nostalgia throughout the first movement, the half-lit eerie waltzing of the second, and obsessive, demonic drive of the Finale, capped by an exorcistic outburst of the *Dies Irae*, left many bewildered. Die-hard Romantics were given only the saxophone second subject of the opening movement to cling to, and modernists were, as ever, maddened by Rachmaninov's refusal to tow the contemporary line. It is only in more recent years that the *Symphonic Dances* have become widely recognized as one of Rachmaninov's crowning achievements.

Before leaving New York to go on tour, he gave a rare insight into his composing methods to the magazine, *The Etude*:

Composing is as essential a part of my being as breathing or eating . . . my constant desire to compose music is actually the urge within me to give tonal expression to my thoughts . . . In my own compositions, no conscious effort has been made to be original, or Romantic, or Nationalistic, or anything else. I write down on paper the music I hear within me, as naturally as possible. I am a Russian composer, and the land of my birth has influenced my temperament and outlook. My music is the product of the temperament, and so it is Russian music; I never consciously attempt to write Russian music, or any other kind of music . . . What I try to do, when writing down my music, is to say simply and directly that which is in my heart when I am composing. If there be love . . . or bitterness, or sadness, or religion, these moods become a part of my music. . . .

By now, America was in the war, brought about by the Japanese attack on Pearl Harbor on 7 December 1941. Rachmaninov made his last commercial recordings, including his *Fourth Concerto* with the Philadelphia Orchestra and Ormandy, set down in a single day, and finally the Liszt transcription of Schubert's song '*Ständchen*'.

Having spent most of his time in America based along the East Coast, Rachmaninov rented a house in Beverly Hills, California, during the summer of 1942. The Horowitzs and Koshetzs lived nearby, so there were plenty of opportunities to play through the two-piano and song repertoire, as well as visit the sights of Hollywood – most memorably, the Disney studios. Rachmaninov enjoyed the atmosphere so much that, against Natalia's advice, he decided to move there, finding the perfect house on Elm Drive. As ever, he took special delight in digging the earth and tending the trees. Meanwhile, news of the war in Mother Russia, where tens of thousands of people were being massacred, filled him with horror. He kept sending messages and parcels to Tatyana in the desperate hope that something might get through.

Rachmaninov's health was causing some concern, and following consultations he was told he was suffering from sclerosis and high blood pressure. He had no choice but to give up concertizing after the next season, which was to mark his 70th birthday. The twenty-two-concert schedule began in Detroit on 12 October 1942. Rachmaninov was clearly on good form, judging by the glowing reviews:

> . . . *There seems to be no flattening of his fingers, no weakening of his attack, no waning of his powers. Rather he seems to defy the idea of old age with a vigour and force that is indeed incredible. The facility with which he can encompass the technical demands of lightning passages in a Liszt bravura piece, for example, is something you can hardly bring your ears to believe.*

Remarkably he was still learning new repertoire, most notably, for this season, Schumann's taxing *Faschingsschwank aus Wien*.

During November he was back in New York for a recital, donating his fee to war relief for Russia as he often did. Then, in the December, he helped the conductor, Dmitri Mitropoulos, prepare for the first New York Philharmonic performances of the *Symphonic Dances*. Mitropoulos's interpretation won the general approval of even the waspish New York critics, as did Rachmaninov's playing of the *Rhapsody*. A reception was even held in his honour, to mark his fifty years as a concert virtuoso. The city would never see him again.

Rachmaninov took a six week 'interval', during which the last official photographs of him were taken by a *Life* magazine photographer. By the middle of January he was in considerable pain, particularly down his left side, and his skin had begun turning yellow. He was losing weight fast and was having severe problems throwing off a stubborn cough. Yet, given his extraordinary resilience in the past, and despite the fact that he still smoked more than forty cigarettes a day, no one seemed unduly alarmed. Having received their final papers granting American citizenship on 1 February, the Rachmaninovs resumed the concert tour at State College, Pennsylvania, two days later.

On 5 February he was in Columbus, Ohio, where the Somovs came to hear him play despite his pleading with them not to. When they met up with him at the intermission, they were greatly distressed by his appearance – he was gaunt and complained of tiredness and weakness, and was clearly aware that his flame was slowly but surely extinguishing. He mentioned not having any flair left for composition and that at least the playing gave him the purpose to go on.

He gave two performances of a *Paganini Rhapsody* / Beethoven *First Concerto* double bill in Chicago during February, which was greeted by uproarious ovations. In absolute agony he carried out engagements in Louisville and then Knoxville on 17 February – the latter because he had had to cancel a recital there some years before and didn't want to disappoint a second time. His sense of duty drove him on to the end. It seems unimaginable that among the works heard that evening from the hands of a dying man was Chopin's highly demanding '*Funeral March*' *Sonata*.

Yet Rachmaninov refused to give in. Travelling to his next venue, in Florida by train, his already dire condition worsened and he was forced to cancel. They stopped in Atlanta, proceeding to New Orleans for a couple of days in the sun, before moving on to Texas on the next stage of the tour. But it was clearly hopeless; Rachmaninov was fading fast. On 22 February, he wrote to Professor Rashevsky: 'The pains in my side seem stronger and I am terribly weak. It's getting harder for me to play. I should see a doctor.'

Rachmaninov and Natalia then made the arduous, three-day train journey back to Los Angeles, where an ambulance whisked him off to hospital. Although initial tests showed nothing, there was little doubt that cancer was the most likely prognosis. Having been discharged, he returned to Elm Drive with a nurse to keep him under observation. Relatives, including Irina, arrived to be by his bedside, which at least provided some relief. They then received the news that he was indeed suffering from an uncontrollable form of cancer – it was decided to keep it from the great man. Small swellings appeared all over his body as the melanoma began to attack his skin. Nothing could be done.

Further comfort was provided by the installation of a radio, and Natalia stayed with him to the end, often reading Pushkin at his request. In the last week of March his condition went rapidly downhill and he slid into a coma. Legend has it that, realizing his end was in sight, the last words he uttered were: 'Good-bye, my hands.'

A cable arrived on 27 March signed by many Soviet composers congratulating him on his coming seventieth birthday – he never saw it. On 28 March at 1.30am, he passed away. Natalia, never fond of the Elm Road house, returned to New York soon after Rachmaninov's death. This explains his burial not in California but in the peaceful cemetery of a Russian Orthodox church in Kensico, a small town a few miles from New York City. Here he lies marked by a simple cross of gleaming white marble, enclosed by an incomplete circle of evergreen hedges and trees.

Of the various tributes made to this giant among men, Joseph Hofmann's, stands out:

> *Rachmaninov was made of steel and gold;*
> *steel in his arms, gold in his heart.*
> *I can never think of this majestic being*
> *without tears in my eyes,*
> *for I not only admired him as a supreme artist,*
> *but I also loved him as a man.*

Rachmaninov lies buried in an aluminium casket, allowing the possibility that one day his remains may be laid to rest in Russia, perhaps in the grounds of the estate that he loved so dearly – Ivanovka.

SERGEI RACHMANINOV:
COMPLETE LIST OF WORKS
AND SELECTED FURTHER READING

Piano piece played to Matvey Pressman (1886, lost)

Arrangement of Tchaikovsky's *'Manfred' Symphony* for piano
duet (1886, lost)

Song without Words in D minor for piano (c.1887)

Four *Pieces* for piano (c.1887)

Three *Nocturnes* for piano (1887–88)

Scherzo in D minor for orchestra (1888)

Esmeralda, opera after Hugo's *Notre Dame de Paris*, sketches in
piano score (1888)

Two Movements (*String Quartet No.1*) for string quartet (c.1889)

Piano Concerto in C minor (unfinished sketch of first movement
scored for two pianos) (1889)

Romance in A minor for violin and piano (c.1880s)

Piece in canonic style in D minor for piano (c.1890)

'At the Gate of the Holy Abode', song for low voice (Lermontov)
(1890)

'I shall tell Nothing', song for low voice (Fet) (1890)

'Again you Leapt, my Heart ', song for high voice (Grekov) (c.1890)

Romance in F minor for cello and piano (1890)

'Deus meus', motet for six-part unaccompanied chorus (c.1890)

Manfred for orchestra (c.1890, lost)

Valse & Romance for one piano, six hands (1890–1)

Suite for orchestra (1891, lost)

'C'était en avril ', song for high voice (Pailleron) (1891)

'Twilight has Fallen', song for high voice (Tolstoy) (1891)

Three *Monologues* (c.1891):

  ◊ *Boris's Aria* for low voice (three versions)

◊ *Pimen's Aria* for high voice (two versions) (this and *Boris's Aria* both from Pushkin's *Boris Godunov*)

◊ *Arbenin's Aria* for low voice (from Lermontov's *Masquerade*)

Arrangement of Tchaikovsky's *The Sleeping Beauty* for piano duet (1891)

Prelude in F for piano (1891)

Arrangement of the '*Russian Boatmen's Song*' for voice and piano (c.1891)

Russian Rhapsody for two pianos (1891)

Piano Concerto No.1 in F sharp minor, Op.1 (1891, revised 1917)

Symphonic movement in D minor (1891)

Prince Rostislav, symphonic poem for orchestra after Tolstoy (1891)

Trio élégiaque (Piano Trio No.1) in G minor (1892)

Aleko, opera in one act after Pushkin's poem *The Gypsies* (1892)

Two Pieces for cello and piano, Op.2 (1892)

Five *Morceaux de fantaisie* for piano, Op.3 (1892)

'*Song of the Disillusioned* ', song for low voice (Rathaus) (c.1893)

'*The Flower has Faded* ', song for high voice (Rathaus) (c.1893)

'*Do you Remember this Evening?*', song for high voice (Tolstoy) (c.1893)

Six Songs, Op.4:

◊ '*Oh stay, my Love, Forsake me not* ', for medium voice (Merezhkovsky) (1892)

◊ '*Morning*', for low voice (Yanov) (1892)

◊ '*In the Silence of the Secret Night* ', for medium voice (Fet) (c.1892)

◊ '*Sing not to me, Beautiful Maiden*', for high voice (Pushkin) (1893)

◊ '*O Thou, my Field* ', for high voice (Tolstoy) (1893)

◊ '*How long, my Friend* ', for high voice (Golenishchev-Kutuzov) (1893)

Fantaisie-tableaux (Suite No.1) for two pianos, Op.5 (1893)

Two Pieces for violin and piano, Op.6 (1893)

The Crag (or *The Rock*), fantasy for orchestra after Lermontov and Chekhov, Op.7 (1893)

Six Songs, Op.8 (1893):

◊ '*The Water Lily*', for medium voice (Heine)

◊ '*Child, Thou art Beautiful as a Flower*', for medium voice (Heine)

◊ '*Brooding*', for medium voice (Shevchenko)

◊ '*I have Grown Fond of Sorrow*', for medium voice (Shevchenko)

◊ '*The Dream*', for high voice (Heine)

◊ '*A Prayer*', for high voice (Goethe)

Trio élégiaque (Piano Trio No.2) in D minor, Op.9 (1893)

'*O Mother of God Vigilantly Praying*', motet for four-part
   unaccompanied mixed chorus (1893)

Seven *Morceaux de salon* for piano, Op.10 (1894)

Romance for piano duet (c.1894)

'*Chorus of Spirits*', from *Don Juan*, for four-part unaccompanied
   chorus (Tolstoy) (c.1894)

Six *Duets* for piano duet, Op.11 (1894)

Capriccio on Gypsy Themes for orchestra, Op.12 (1894)

Symphony No.1 in D minor, Op.13 (1895)

Twelve Songs, Op.14 (1896, except No.1, composed 1894):

◊ '*I wait for Thee*', for high voice (Davidova)

◊ '*The Island* ', for high voice (Shelley)

◊ '*How Few the Joys*', for low voice (Fet)

◊ '*I was with Her*', for medium voice (Koltsov)

◊ '*Midsummer Nights*', for high voice (Rathaus)

◊ '*How Everyone Loves Thee*', for medium voice (Tolstoy)

◊ '*Believe me not, Friend* ', for high voice (Tolstoy)

◊ '*Oh, do not Grieve*', for medium voice (Apukhtin)

◊ '*She is Lovely as the Noon*', for medium voice (Minsky)

◊ '*Love's Flame*', for low voice (Minsky)

◊ '*Spring Waters*', for high voice (Tyutchev)

◊ '*Tis Time*', for low voice (Nadson)

Six Choruses for women's or children's voices and piano, Op.15
   (1895–96):

◊ '*Be Praised* ' (Nekrasov)

◊ '*The Night* ' (Lodyzhensky)

◊ '*The Pine Tree*' (Lermontov)

◊ '*The Dreaming Waves*' (Romanov)

◊ '*Captivity*' (Tsyganov)

◊ '*The Angel* ' (Lermontov)

Two *Movements* (*String Quartet No.2*) for string quartet (c.1896)

Four *Improvisations* (with Arensky, Glazunov & Taneyev) for
   piano (1896)

Six *Moments musicaux* for piano, Op.16 (1896)

Arrangemement of Glazunov's *Sixth Symphony* for piano duet
   (1897)

Morceau de fantaisie in G minor for piano (1899)

'*Were you Hiccupping?* ', song for low voice (Vyazemsky) (1899)

'*Panteley the Healer*', for four-part unaccompanied mixed chorus (Tolstoy) (1899)

'*Night* ', song for medium voice (Rathaus) (1900)

Transcription of the *Minuet* from Bizet's *L' Arlésienne* for piano (1901, revised 1922)

Suite No.2 for two pianos, Op.17 (1901)

Piano Concerto No.2 in C minor, Op.18 (1901)

Cello Sonata in G minor, Op.19 (1901)

Spring, cantata for baritone, chorus and orchestra, Op.20 (Nekrasov) (1902)

Twelve Songs, Op.21 (1902, except No.1, composed 1900):
- ◊ '*Fate*', for low voice (Apukhtin)
- ◊ '*By the Grave*', for low voice (Nadson)
- ◊ '*Twilight* ', for high voice (Guyot)
- ◊ '*The Answer*', for high voice (Hugo)
- ◊ '*Lilacs*', for high voice (Beketova)
- ◊ '*Loneliness*', for high voice (de Musset)
- ◊ '*How Fair this Spot* ', for high voice (Galina)
- ◊ '*On the Death of a Linnet* ', for medium voice (Zhukovsky)
- ◊ '*Melody*', for high voice (Nadson)
- ◊ '*Before the Image*', for medium voice (Golenishchev-Kutuzov)
- ◊ '*No Prophet I* ', for high voice (Kruglov)
- ◊ '*How Painful for Me*', for high voice (Galina)

Variations on a Theme of Chopin for piano, Op.22 (1903)

Ten *Preludes* for piano, Op.23 (1903, except No.5, composed 1901)

The Miserly Knight, opera in three scenes based on Pushkin's poem, Op.24 (1905)

Francesca da Rimini, opera in two scenes, a prologue and epilogue based on Dante's *Inferno*, Op.25 (1905)

Polka italienne for piano duet (c.1906)

Fifteen Songs, Op.26 (1906):
- ◊ '*The Heart's Secret* ', for medium voice (Tolstoy)
- ◊ '*He Took All from Me*', for medium voice (Tyutchev)
- ◊ '*Let us Rest* ', for low voice (Chekov)
- ◊ '*Two Partings*', duet for soprano and baritone voices (Koltsov)
- ◊ '*Beloved, let us Fly*', for high voice (Golenishchev-Kutuzov)
- ◊ '*Christ is Risen*', for medium voice (Merezhkovsky)
- ◊ '*To the Children*', for medium voice (Khomyakov)

- ◆ *'I beg for Mercy'*, for high voice (Merezhkovsky)
- ◆ *'Again I am Alone'*, for high voice (Shevchenko)
- ◆ *'Before my Window'*, for high voice (Galina)
- ◆ *'The Fountain'*, for high voice (Tyutchev)
- ◆ *'Night is Mournful '*, for high voice (Bunin)
- ◆ *'When Yesterday We Met '*, for medium voice (Polonsky)
- ◆ *'The Ring'*, for medium voice (Koltsov)
- ◆ *'All Things Depart '*, for low voice (Rathaus)

Monna Vanna, unfinished opera based on Maeterlinck's play (one act in vocal score) (1907)

Symphony No.2 in E minor, Op.27 (1907)

Piano Sonata No.1 in D minor, Op.28 (1907)

'Letter to K.S. Stanislavsky', song for low voice (1908)

The Isle of the Dead, symphonic poem for orchestra based on Böcklin's painting, Op.29 (1909)

Piano Concerto No.3 in D minor, Op.30 (1909)

Liturgy of St John Chrysostom for four-part unaccompanied chorus, Op.31 (1910)

Thirteen *Preludes* for piano, Op.32 (1910)

Polka de VR for piano based on Behr's polka *Lachtäubchen* (1911)

Six *Etudes-tableaux* for piano, Op.33 (1911)

Fourteen Songs, Op.34 (1912, except No.7, composed 1910, revised 1912):

- ◆ *'The Muse'*, for high voice (Pushkin)
- ◆ *'The Soul's Concealment '*, for low voice (Korinfsky)
- ◆ *'The Storm'*, for high voice (Pushkin)
- ◆ *'The Migrant Wind '*, for high voice (Balmont)
- ◆ *'Arion'*, for high voice (Pushkin)
- ◆ *'The Rising of Lazurus'*, for low voice (Khomyakov)
- ◆ *'It Cannot Be'*, for medium voice (Maykov)
- ◆ *'Music'*, for medium voice (Polonsky)
- ◆ *'The Poet '*, for medium voice (Tyutchev)
- ◆ *'I Remember That Day'*, for high voice (Tyutchev)
- ◆ *'The Peasant '*, for low voice (Fet)
- ◆ *'What Happiness'*, for high voice (Fet)
- ◆ *'Dissonance'*, for high voice (Polonsky)
- ◆ *'Vocalise'*, for high voice (wordless)

The Bells, based on Balmont's adaptation of Poe's poem, for soprano, tenor, baritone, chorus and orchestra, Op.35 (1913)

Piano Sonata No.2 in B flat minor, Op.36 (1913, revised 1931)

Transcription of the song '*Lilacs*', Op.21, No.5 for piano
  (c.1913)

All-Night Vigil (Vespers) for four-part unaccompanied mixed
  chorus, Op.37 (1915)

'*From the Gospel of St John*', song for low voice (1915)

Six Songs for high voice, Op.38 (1916):
  ◊ '*In my Garden*' (Isaakyan)
  ◊ '*To Her*' (Bely)
  ◊ '*Daisies*' (Severyanin)
  ◊ '*The Rat Catcher*' (Bryusov)
  ◊ '*The Dream*' (Sologub)
  ◊ '*The Quest*' (Balmont)

Nine *Etudes-tableaux* for piano, Op.39 (1916–17)

Piece in D minor for piano (1917)

Oriental Sketch for piano (1917)

Fragments for piano (1917)

Transcription of Smith's *The Star-Spangled Banner* for piano
  (c.1918)

Cadenza to Liszt's *Hungarian Rhapsody No.2* for piano (c.1919)

Transcription of the wordless song '*Vocalise*', Op.34, No.14 for
  orchestra (c.1919)

Arrangement of folksong '*O Apple Tree, O Apple Tree*' for low
  voice (1920)

Transcription of Kreisler's *Liebesleid* for piano (c.1921)

Transcription of the song '*Daisies*', Op.38, No.3 for piano
  (c.1922, revised 1940)

Transcription of the *Gopak* from Mussorgsky's *Sarochintsky Fair*
  for piano (1924)

Transcription of Kreisler's *Liebesfreud* for piano (c.1925)

Transcription of the song '*Wohin?*' from Schubert's '*Die schöne
  Müllerin*' for piano (1925)

Arrangement of '*Powder and Paint* ', folksong for voice and piano
  (1925)

Piano Concerto No.4 in G minor, Op.40 (1926, final revised 1941)

Three *Russian Songs* for chorus and orchestra, Op.41 (1926)

Transcription of the *Gopak* from Mussorgsky's *Sarochintsky Fair*
  for violin and piano (1926)

Transcription of *The Flight of the Bumblebee* from Rimsky's *Legend
  of Tsar Sultan* for piano (c.1929)

Variations on a Theme of Corelli for piano, Op.42 (1931)

Transcription of three movements from Bach's *Solo Violin Partita in E* for piano (1933)

Transcription of the Scherzo from Mendelssohn's *A Midsummer Night's Dream* for piano (c.1933)

Rhapsody on a Theme of Paganini for piano and orchestra, Op.43 (1934)

Symphony No.3 in A minor, Op.44 (1936)

Symphonic Dances for orchestra (also in version for two pianos, Op.45a), Op.45 (1940)

Transcription of Tchaikovsky's song '*Lullaby*', Op.16, No.1 for piano (1941)

◆

SELECTED FURTHER READING

Although very few comprehensive studies on Rachmaninov have ever appeared in English, those that have are invariably of a very high standard. The following books are all pioneering works of their kind and will fully repay further investigation and study.

- Sergei Bertensson & Jay Leyda: *Sergei Rachmaninoff: A Lifetime in Music* (George Allen & Unwin, 1965).
- John Culshaw: *Sergei Rachmaninov* (Dobson, 1949)
- Barrie Martyn: *Rachmaninoff: Composer, Pianist, Conductor* (Scolar Press 1990)
- Geoffrey Norris: *Rachmaninoff* (Dent/Oxford University Press, rev. 1993)
- Robert Palmieri: *Sergei Vasil'evich Rachmaninoff: A Guide to Research* (Garland, 1985)
- Patrick Piggott: *Rachmaninov* (Faber, 1978)
- Patrick Piggott: *Rachmaninov Orchestral Music* (BBC, 1973)
- Robert Threlfall & Geoffrey Norris: *Catalogue of the Compositions of Sergei Rachmaninoff* (Scolar Press, 1982)
- Robert Walker: *Rachmaninoff* (Omnibus, 1984)

SERGEI RACHMANINOV: RECOMMENDED RECORDINGS

T he following list represents a distinguished cross-section of inter-
pretative approaches from the wealth of available recordings.
Where different artists have been coupled together on the same
CD, the relevant artists and works are shown by an asterisk (*).

HISTORICAL

**The Complete RCA Victor Rachmaninov Recordings
(including Piano Concertos Nos.1–4, Paganini Rhapsody,
Symphony No.3, The Isle of the Dead, Preludes,
Etudes-tableaux, transcriptions, shorter piano works, as
well as numerous works by other composers)**
♦ Sergei Rachmaninov (piano/conductor), Philadelphia
  Orchestra / Eugene Ormandy, Leopold Stokowski
  ⊗ RCA 09026 61265-2 (10 discs, mono)

Piano Concerto No.3 in D minor, Op.30
♦ Emil Gilels (piano), Paris Conservatoire Orchestra / André
  Cluytens ⊗ Testament SBT 1029 (mono, coupled with Saint-
  Saëns: *Piano Concerto No.2*; Shostakovich: *Prelude & Fugue in D*)

**The Isle of the Dead, Op.29; Symphony No.3 in A
minor, Op.44; Vocalise, Op.34, No.14**
♦ Philadelphia Orchestra / Sergei Rachmaninov
  ⊗ Pearl GEMMCD 9414 (mono)

'Rachmaninov plays Rachmaninov' on RCA
♦ Sergei Rachmaninov (piano) ⊗ RCA GD 87766 (mono)

'Rachmaninov plays Rachmaninov' on Ampico
Piano-Rolls

♦ Sergei Rachmaninov (piano) ⊗ Decca 425 964-2 (stereo)

ORCHESTRAL

Piano Concertos

Piano Concertos Nos.1–4;
Rhapsody on a Theme of Paganini, Op.43

♦ Howard Shelley (piano), Scottish National Orchestra /
Bryden Thomson ⊗ Chandos CHAN 8882/3 (2 discs)

Piano Concertos Nos.1–4;
Rhapsody on a Theme of Paganini, Op.43

♦ Earl Wild (piano), Royal Philharmonic Orchestra / Jascha
Horenstein ⊗ Chandos CHAN 8521/2 (2 discs)

Piano Concertos Nos.1–4

♦ Vladimir Ashkenazy (piano), London Symphony Orchestra
/ André Previn ⊗ Decca 444 839-2 (2 discs)

Piano Concertos Nos.1–4

♦ Jean-Philippe Collard (piano), Toulouse Capitole
Orchestra / Michel Plasson ⊗ EMI CZS7 67419-2 (2 discs)

Piano Concerto No.1 in F sharp minor, Op.1;
Rhapsody on a Theme of Paganini, Op.43

♦ Mikhail Pletnev (piano), Philharmonia Orchestra / Libor
Pešek ⊗ Virgin VC7 59506-2

Piano Concerto No.1 in F sharp minor, Op.1

♦ Byron Janis (piano), Moscow Philharmonic Orchestra /
Kyril Kondrashin ⊗ Philips Mercury 434 333-2

Piano Concerto No.2 in C minor, Op.18

♦ Van Cliburn (piano), Chicago Symphony Orchestra / Fritz
Reiner ⊗ RCA 09026 61961-2 (coupled with Beethoven: *Piano
Concerto No.5*)

Piano Concerto No.2 in C minor, Op.18;
***Piano Concerto No.3 in D minor, Op.30;**
Preludes, Op.3, No.2 & Op.23, No.5
♦ Byron Janis (piano), Minneapolis Symphony Orchestra,
  *London Symphony Orchestra / Antal Dorati
    ⊗ Philips Mercury 432 759-2

Piano Concerto No.3 in D minor, Op.30
♦ Martha Argerich (piano), Berlin Radio Symphony
  Orchestra / Riccardo Chailly ⊗ Philips 446 673-2 (coupled with
  Tchaikovsky: *Piano Concerto No.1*)

Piano Concerto No.4 in G minor, Op.40 (revised 1941)
♦ Arturo Benedetti Michelangeli (piano), Philharmonia
  Orchestra / Ettore Gracis ⊗ EMI CDC7 49326-2 (coupled with
  Ravel: *Piano Concerto in G*)

***Piano Concerto No.4 in G minor, Op.40 (revised 1927);**
Monna Vanna: Act I (orchestrated by Buketoff)
♦ *William Black (piano), Sherrill Milnes (Guido), Seth
  McCoy (Marco), Blythe Walker (Monna Vanna), Icelandic
  Opera Chorus, Iceland Symphony Orchestra / Igor
  Buketoff ⊗ Chandos CHAN 8987

Symphonies / Symphonic poems

Symphonies Nos.1–3; The Isle of the Dead, Op.29;
Symphonic Dances, Op.45; Vocalise, Op.34, No.14;
Aleko: Intermezzo; Women's Dance
♦ London Symphony Orchestra / André Previn
    ⊗ EMI CMS7 64530–2 (3 discs)

Symphonies Nos.1–3; The Crag, Op.7
♦ Berlin Philharmonic Orchestra / Lorin Maazel
    ⊗ DG 445 590-2 (2 discs)

Symphony No.1 in D minor, Op.13;
The Isle of the Dead, Op.29
♦ Concertgebouw Orchestra / Vladimir Ashkenazy
    ⊗ Decca 436 479-2

Symphony No.1 in D minor, Op.13;
Five Etudes-tableaux (orchestrated by Respighi)
♦   BBC Welsh Symphony Orchestra / Tadaaki Otaka
    ⊗ Nimbus NI 5311

Symphony No.2 in E minor, Op.27; Scherzo in D minor;
Vocalise, Op.34, No.14
♦   St Petersburg Philharmonic Orchestra / Mariss Jansons
    ⊗ EMI CDC5 55140V-2

Symphony No.2 in E minor, Op.27;
Vocalise, Op.34, No.14
♦   Royal Philharmonic Orchestra / Andrew Litton
    ⊗ Virgin VC7 59548-2

Symphony No.3 in A minor, Op.44;
Symphonic Dances, Op.45
♦   Baltimore Symphony Orchestra / David Zinman
    ⊗ Telarc CD 80331

Symphony No.3 in A minor, Op.44
♦   London Symphony Orchestra / André Previn
    ⊗ EMI CDM7 69564-2 (coupled with Shostakovich: *Symphony No.6*)

'Youth' Symphony in D minor; Symphony No.2
in E minor, Op.27
♦   Concertgebouw Orchestra / Vladimir Ashkenazy
    ⊗ Decca 436 480-2

Caprice bohémien (Capriccio on Gypsy Themes), Op.12;
Symphonic Dances, Op.45; Aleko: Women's Dance;
Men's Dance
♦   Philharmonia Orchestra / Neeme Järvi
    ⊗ Chandos CHAN 9081

Prince Rostislav;
***Piano Concerto No.3 in D minor, Op.30**
♦   *Berndt Glemser (piano), Irish National Symphony
    Orchestra / Jerzy Maksymiuk   ⊗ Naxos 8.550666

Symphonic Dances, Op.45;
Symphony No.3 in A minor, Op.44

♦ Concertgebouw Orchestra / Vladimir Ashkenazy
⊗ Decca 436 481–2

Symphonic Dances, Op.45

♦ Philadelphia Orchestra / Eugene Ormandy
⊗ Sony SBK 48279 (coupled with Offenbach: *Gaîté parisienne*;
Smetana: *Bartered Bride*, & *Dances*)

Orchestral transcriptions of Trio élégiaque No.2, Op.9;
Variations on a Theme of Corelli, Op.42;
Vocalise, Op.34, No.14

♦ Detroit Symphony Orch. / Neeme Järvi ⊗ Chandos CHAN 9261

SOLO PIANO

The Complete Piano Works

♦ Howard Shelley (piano) ⊗ Hyperion CDS 44041/8 (8 discs)

Canon in E minor; Morceaux de fantaisie, Op.3, Nos.1, 3, 4

♦ Margaret Fingerhut (piano) ⊗ Chandos CHAN 9218
(coupled with a programme of popular Russian piano miniatures)

Etudes-tableaux, Opp.33 & 39 (complete)

♦ Howard Shelley (piano) ⊗ Hyperion CDA 66091

Etudes-Tableaux, Opp.33 & 39 (complete)

♦ Gordon Fergus-Thompson (piano) ⊗ ASV CDDCA 789

Etudes-tableaux, Op.39;
Variations on a Theme of Corelli, Op.42

♦ Vladimir Ashkenazy (piano) ⊗ Decca 417 671-2

Moments musicaux, Op.16; Morceaux de salon, Op.10

♦ Howard Shelley (piano) ⊗ Hyperion CDA 66184

Morceaux de fantaisie, Op.3; Preludes, Op.23

♦ Howard Shelley (piano) ⊗ Hyperion CDA 66081

Preludes (complete), **Op.3, 23 & 32; Piano Sonata No.2**
- Vladimir Ashkenazy (piano) ⊗ Decca 443 841–2 (2 discs)

Preludes, Op.32; Prelude in F; Prelude in D minor
- Howard Shelley (piano) ⊗ Hyperion CDA 66082

Piano Sonata No.1 in D minor, Op.28; Piano Sonata No.2 in B flat minor, Op.36 (1913 version)
- Gordon Fergus-Thompson (piano) ⊗ Kingdom KCLCD 2007

Piano Sonata No.1 in D minor, Op.28; Piano Sonata No.2 in B flat minor, Op.36 (1931 version)
- Howard Shelley (piano) ⊗ Hyperion CDA 66047

Variations on a Theme of Chopin, Op.22; Variations on a Theme of Corelli, Op.42
- Howard Shelley (piano) ⊗ Hyperion CDA 66009

Piano Transcriptions
- Howard Shelley (piano) ⊗ Hyperion CDA 66486

Piano Transcriptions
- Janice Weber (piano) ⊗ Carlton PCD 1051

Twelve Song Transcriptions
- Earl Wild (piano) ⊗ Dell'Arte CDDBS 7001

Collection
- Sviatoslav Richter (piano) ⊗ Olympia OCD 337

Collection
- Vladimir Horowitz (piano) ⊗ Sony SK 53472
  (coupled with pieces by Scriabin and Medtner)

VOCAL

The Complete Songs
- Elisabeth Söderstrom (soprano), Vladimir Ashkenazy (piano) ⊗ Decca 436 920-2

The Complete Songs, Vol.1: Six Songs, Op.4; Six Songs, Op.8; Twelve Songs, Op.14; Eight settings without opus
- ⊗ Chandos CHAN 9405

The Complete Songs, Vol.2: Twelve Songs, Op.21; Fifteen Songs, Op.26; 'Were you Hiccupping?'; Night
- ⊗ Chandos CHAN 9451

The Complete Songs, Vol.3: Fourteen Songs, Op.34; Six Songs, Op.38; Letter to K.S. Stanislavsky; Powder and Paint Song
- ⊗ Chandos CHAN 9477

All three volumes: Joan Rodgers (soprano), Maria Popescu (mezzo), Alexandre Naoumenko (tenor), Sergei Leiferkus (bass), Howard Shelley (piano)

All-Night Vigil (Vespers), Op.37
- Jeanne Polvtsova (mezzo), Sergei Rokozitsa (tenor), Leningrad Glinka Academy Chorus / Vladislav Chernushenko ⊗ Russian Disc RDCD 11016

All-Night Vigil (Vespers), Op.37
- Karl Dent (tenor), Robert Shaw Festival Singers / Robert Shaw ⊗ Telarc CD 80172

The Bells, Op.35; three Russian Songs, Op.41
- Natalia Troitskaya (soprano), Ryszard Karczykowski (tenor), Tom Krause (baritone), Concertgebouw Orchestra and Chorus / Vladimir Ashkenazy ⊗ Decca 436 482-2

The Bells, Op.35
- Sheila Armstrong (soprano), Robert Tear (tenor), John Shirley-Quirk (baritone), London Symphony Orchestra and Chorus / André Previn ⊗ EMI CDM7 63114-2 (coupled with Prokofiev: *Alexander Nevsky*)

Six Choruses, Op.15
- Bolshoi Children's Chorus / Vladimir Krainev ⊗ Chant du Monde LDC 288 013

**Deus meus; Choral Concerto; Six Choruses, Op.15;
Panteley the Healer; Two Sacred Songs; Six Songs, Op.38**
- ◆ Vocal Ensemble C sharp minor / Elger Niels
  - ⊗ Syncoop 5753 CD 160

**Liturgy of St John Chrysostom, Op.31;
O Mother of God Vigilantly Praying;
Chorus of Spirits (Don Juan); Panteley the Healer**
- ◆ Russian State Symphony Cappella / Valery Polyansky
  - ⊗ Claves CD 50-9304–5 (2 discs)

Liturgy of St John Chrysostom, Op.31
- ◆ St Petersburg Chamber Choir / Nikolai Korniev
  - ⊗ Philips 442 776-2

Spring (cantata), Op.20; The Bells, Op.35
- ◆ Elena Ustinova (soprano), Kurt Westi (tenor), Jorma
  Hynninen (baritone), Danish National Radio Symphony
  Orch. and Choir / Dmitri Kitajenko ⊗ Chandos CHAN 8966

OPERA

Aleko
- ◆ Vladimir Matorine (Aleko), Natasha Erassova (Zemfira),
  Bolshoi Soloists, Russian State Choir, Studio Orchestra /
  Andrey Chistiakov ⊗ Chant du Monde 288 079

The Miserly Knight, Op.24
- ◆ Mikhail Krutikov (Baron), Vladimir Kudriashov (Albert),
  Bolshoi Soloists, Studio Orchestra / Andrey Chistiakov
  - ⊗ Chant du Monde 288 080

Francesca da Rimini, Op.25
- ◆ Vladimir Matorin (Lanciotto), Marina Lapina (Francesca),
  Vitaly Taratchenko (Paolo), Bolshoi Soloists, Studio
  Orchestra / Andrey Chistiakov ⊗ Chant du Monde 288 081

or all 3 operas as above in one boxed set
- ◆ ⊗ CMX 388053 (3 discs)

CHAMBER

Cello Sonata in G minor, Op.19
♦ Yo-Yo Ma (cello), Emmanuel Ax (piano)
  ⊗ Sony SK 46486 (coupled with Prokofiev: *Cello Sonata*, Op.119)

Complete Music for Two Pianos, Piano Duet & *Piano/ Six Hands
♦ Thorson & Thurber (pianos), *David Gardiner (piano)
  ⊗ Paula PACD 46 (2 discs)

Two-Piano Music: Suites Nos.1 & 2; Russian Rhapsody; Symphonic Dances, Op.45; *Eight Etudes-tableaux, Op.33; *Variations on a Theme of Corelli, Op.42
♦ *Vladimir Ashkenazy, André Previn (pianos)
  ⊗ Decca 444 845-2 (2 discs)

Two Cello Pieces, Op.2
♦ Alexander Ivashkin (cello), Ingrid Wahlberg (piano)
  ⊗ ODE CDMANU 1426 (coupled with popular Russian cello works)

Romance in F minor for cello and piano
♦ Julian Lloyd-Webber (cello), John Lenehan (piano)
  ⊗ Philips 434 917-2 (coupled with popular arrangements of Delius, Brahms, Schumann, Grieg, etc.)

'String Quartets' Nos.1 & 2 (both unfinished); *Piano Trio No.2 in D minor, Op.9
♦ Artur Balsam (piano), Budapest String Quartet
  ⊗ Bridge 9063 (mono)

Trio élégiaque No.1 in G minor; Trio élégiaque No.2 in D minor, Op.9
♦ Borodin Trio ⊗ Chandos CHAN 8341

Index

THE
CLASSIC *f*M
GUIDE TO
CLASSICAL MUSIC

JEREMY NICHOLAS

'... *a fascinating and accessible guide ... it will provide
an informative and illuminating source of insight
for everybody from the beginner to the musicologist.*'

Sir Edward Heath

The Classic fM Guide to Classical Music opens with a masterly
history of classical music, illustrated with charts and lifelines, and
is followed by a comprehensive guide to more than 500 composers. There are major entries detailing the lives and works of the
world's most celebrated composers, as well as concise biographies
of more than 300 others.

This invaluable companion to classical music combines extensive
factual detail with fascinating anecdotes, and an insight into the
historical and musical influences of the great composers. It also
contains reviews and recommendations of the best works, and
extensive cross-references to lesser-known composers. Jeremy
Nicholas's vibrant, informative and carefully researched text is
complemented by photographs and cartoons, and is designed for
easy reference, with a comprehensive index.

£19.99   ISBN: 1 85793 760 0   Hardback
£9.99   ISBN: 1 86205 051 1   Paperback

CLASSIC *f*M
COMPACT COMPANIONS

CHOPIN, PUCCINI, ROSSINI, TCHAIKOVSKY

In association with *Classic fM* and *Philips Classics*, this revolutionary new series, **Compact Companions**, is a stylish package of book and compact disc. Each title provides the ultimate prelude to the lives and works of the most popular composers of classical music.

These composers' extraordinary, eventful lives and their powerful, moving music make them the ideal subjects for combined reading and listening. Written by respected authors, the texts provide a comprehensive introduction to the life and work of the composer, and each includes a richly illustrated biography, a complete list of works and a definitive list of recommended recordings. The accompanying CD combines both favourite and less-well-known pieces, recorded by artists of world renown.

Chopin
Christopher Headington
ISBN: 1 85793 655 8

Puccini
Jonathon Brown
ISBN: 1 85793 660 4

Rossini
David Mountfield
ISBN: 1 85793 665 5

Tchaikovsky
David Nice
ISBN: 1 85793 670 1

£9.99 (inc. VAT) each companion

These books can be ordered direct from the publisher.
Please contact the Marketing Department.
But try your bookshop first.

CLASSIC *f*M
LIFELINES

With 4.8 million listeners every week, *Classic fM* is now the most listened-to national commercial radio station in the UK. With the launch of *Classic fM Lifelines*, Pavilion Books and *Classic fM* are creating an affordable series of elegantly designed short biographies that will put everyone's favourite composers into focus.

Written with enthusiasm and in a highly accessible style, the *Classic fM Lifelines* series will become the Everyman of musical biographies. Titles for the series have been chosen from *Classic fM*'s own listener surveys of the most popular composers.

TITLES PUBLISHED:

Johannes Brahms
Jonathon Brown
ISBN: 1 85793 967 0

Claude Debussy
Jonathon Brown
ISBN: 1 85793 972 7

Edward Elgar
David Nice
ISBN: 1 85793 977 8

Gustav Mahler
Julian Haylock
ISBN: 1 85793 982 4

Sergei Rachmaninov
Julian Haylock
ISBN: 1 85793 944 1

Franz Schubert
Stephen Jackson
ISBN: 1 85793 987 5

£4.99 each book

FORTHCOMING TITLES:

- ♦ *J.S. Bach*
- ♦ *Ludwig van Beethoven*
- ♦ *Benjamin Britten*

- ♦ *Joseph Haydn*
- ♦ *Dmitri Shostakovich*
- ♦ *Ralph Vaughan Williams*

CLASSIC *f*M
LIFELINES

To purchase any of the books in the *Classic fM Lifelines* series
simply fill in the order form below and post or fax it,
together with your remittance, to the address below.

Please send the titles ticked below
(*published spring 1997)

Johannes Brahms	☐	*J.S. Bach	☐
Claude Debussy	☐	*Ludwig van Beethoven	☐
Edward Elgar	☐	*Benjamin Britten	☐
Gustav Mahler	☐	*Joseph Haydn	☐
Sergei Rachmaninov	☐	*Dmitri Shostakovich	☐
Franz Schubert	☐	*Ralph Vaughan Williams	☐

Number of titles @ £4.99 _____ Value: £_____
Add 10% of total value for postage and packing   Value: £_____
Total value of order: £_____

I enclose a cheque (UK only) payable to Pavilion Books Ltd ☐

OR

Please charge my credit card account ☐

I wish to pay by: Visa ☐ MasterCard ☐ Access ☐ American Express ☐

Card number ☐☐☐☐☐☐☐☐☐☐☐☐☐☐☐☐☐☐☐

Signature_____ Expiry Date_____
Name _____
Address _____
_____
_____ Postcode_____

Please send your order to: Marketing Department, Pavilion Books Ltd,
26 Upper Ground, London SE1 9PD, or fax for quick dispatch to:
Marketing Department, 0171-620 0042.